W9-BKG-715

Defining the Really Great Boss

Defining the Really Great Boss

M. David Dealy with Andrew R. Thomas

Foreword by Bill Lindig

 PRAEGER

Westport, Connecticut
London

Library of Congress Cataloging-in-Publication Data

Dealy, M. David.
   Defining the really great boss / M. David Dealy with Andrew R. Thomas ;
foreword by Bill Lindig.
   p. cm.
   Includes bibliographical references and index.
   ISBN 0-275-98037-5 (alk. paper)
   1. Supervision of employees. 2. Supervisors. 3. Personnel management.
4. Leadership. I. Thomas, Andrew R. II. Title.
HF5549.12.D43   2004
658.3'02—dc22   2003062432

British Library Cataloguing in Publication Data is available.

Library of Congress Catalog Card Number: 2003062432
ISBN 0-275-98037-5

First published in 2004

Praeger Publishers, 88 Post Road West, Westport, CT 06881
An imprint of Greenwood Publishing Group, Inc.
www.praeger.com

Printed in the United States of America

The paper used in this book complies with the
Permanent Paper Standard issued by the National
Information Standards Organization (Z39.48-1984).

10 9 8 7 6 5 4 3 2 1

ACC Library Services
Austin, Texas

To my father, who, as many of his employees said,
was a really great boss.

Contents

Foreword

The world is full of organizations that operate successfully from a business or financial perspective. Many fail, however, as employers. For much of the last hundred years, being a successful business was good enough. The organization survives, makes money, and grows enough to stay around. Today, however, factors are converging to directly challenge this paradigm. The inevitable forces of globalization, information technology, and "free agent" employees are compelling organizations of all sizes to continually evaluate what they are doing and how.

When it comes to leadership, far too many American organizations follow the same "cookie cutter" formulas for bringing them closer to working successfully with their people. The latest management recipes, human resources strategies, or conflict-resolution formulas are all standard, acceptable ways of conducting oneself in today's marketplace. In each of these cases, however, great effort is put forth but the results come up short.

The quest for greatness for those charged with leading America's businesses, nonprofits, and public institutions is seemingly an elusive one. Still, it doesn't have to be that way. It is possible to be a great boss in today's world. It isn't easy, but it can be done.

This book is a big step forward in helping bosses from every kind of organization move beyond mediocrity and toward greatness. The principles set forth are applicable to almost every environment a boss will confront during his or her career. These are simple, yet powerful guidelines that bosses can use to set themselves apart and make the kind of impact today's organizations sorely need.

Bill Lindig
CEO, SYSCO

1

What This Book Is About

The leaders I met, whatever walk of life they were from, whatever institutions they were presiding over, always referred back to a something that happened to them that was personally difficult, even traumatic, something that made them feel that desperate sense of hitting bottom—as something they thought was almost a necessity. It's as if at that moment the iron entered their soul; that moment created the resilience that leaders need.
—Warren G. Bennis

Dr. Phil calls them "defining moments." I had one on the morning of February 1, 1996. That day and the following year after will remain permanently seared into my mind, heart, and soul. I was in Springfield, Missouri, to perform a typical field operations audit. My pager went off just about the time I was walking into our office building. I called our operations center in the Chicago suburb of Schaumburg and spoke with Danny Reynolds, our general superintendent. The conversation started out bad and got worse.

"Dave, I hate to be the one to have to tell you this, but one of our trains just made an emergency call from Cajon Pass. They said the train was out of control going down a steep grade and they were going to jump. That's all we know. We have alerted the police and ambulance teams and they are responding. All we can do now is wait."

This was unbelievable. How could this be happening? We had just had a runaway train accident at this same location a year earlier. One of our trains had lost its air brakes and had collided with a loaded coal train that was stopped ahead. The engineer and conductor had jumped seconds prior to impact at a speed we estimated was in excess of 35 miles per hour. The collision was horrific. The locomotives were engulfed in flames.

About 15 minutes had passed since I had first spoken with Danny. I called him back on the hot line, and I could sense a great degree of gravity in his voice. "We lost contact with the crew. We have received reports from the sheriff that there was a large explosion with a big fireball. It looks like the entire train left the track and is in a pile. Our crew members are missing."

I quickly chartered a jet and flew the three hours to Ontario Airport in Southern California. When I finally arrived at the scene, I learned that the engineer had been rescued from the burning locomotive by nearby ranchers. The bodies of the other two crew members had been discovered near the wreckage.

The entire site was closed to all but emergency response personnel. Just like the previous year, we had the interstate closed. The tracks run parallel to Interstate 15, which is the main route between Los Angeles and Las Vegas. Interstate 40 breaks off east of there at Barstow. This forms one of the major connections between the huge population mass of the Southwest and the Midwest. Our accident had it shut down. We were on national news, and things were getting real tough. Moreover, I seemed to have all of state and federal agencies—including the National Transportation Safety Board, the Department of Transportation, and the California Public Utilities Commission—coming down on me trying to conclude what had happened.

Our engineer had been badly injured. We all wanted to talk to him, including the news media. To make matters worse, immediately after a closed-to-the-public NTSB briefing, a local politician, looking only to get his mug in front of the cameras, announced to the press that the engineer was at fault. His comments, although great fodder for the cameras, were disingenuous and simply not true.

The media feeding frenzy was insatiable. We had to move the engineer to three different hospitals and finally checked him in at a fourth under a false name. We were able to speak to him long enough to understand that he was not at fault, but the fire with the media had already been lit. And, like the four locomotives and 57 freight cars up on the mountain, it was blazing.

It is standard practice in major train wrecks not to comment on cause. Many times it takes days to put the pieces together, and by that time it is no longer news. We are used to saying that the cause is under investigation and letting the story die a natural death below the fold on page 10. However, this one was not going away. The interstate was closed for almost three days. Hundreds of thousands of commuters were inconvenienced. Days later, we were still front page and getting 30 seconds at the top of every hour on CNN.

The chief concern for me was our engineer. He was being blamed for an accident that killed two of his fellow employees, shut down a major highway artery for three days, and posed a serious contamination threat to one of America's largest metropolitan areas. Something needed to be done.

Despite the fact that standard procedure and jurisdictional protocol were against me, I believed that I had to act. I rented a ballroom at a nearby hotel and assembled all our employees, their families, and the union leadership. I told this group that although the media and the irresponsible politician had blamed our engineer, we had determined that he was not at fault. In fact, based on what we knew at the time, we concluded that he had done everything he could have to stop the train. Just like the wreck that had occurred just over a year before, something had caused the train's brakes to fail on all but the cars nearest to the locomotives. This was most disconcerting, I explained, because in this case the train was equipped with a new piece of technology that should have allowed the brakes to be set from the rear of the train using a radio-controlled device. For whatever reason, the new device was not functioning properly.

I stated repeatedly that our train crew was not responsible. I said that management was taking full responsibility. I related that our prayers were with the engineer and his family as well as the families of the two crewmen fatally injured in the accident.

I knew in my heart and in my mind that this was the right thing to do. Needless to say, it was a welcome surprise to our employees and the unions. However, doing the right thing would later expose me to civil lawsuits and the serious threat of a criminal indictment for second-degree murder. For the next year I lived under the very real fear that I might be spending a large portion of the rest of my life in prison.

In the immediate days and weeks following the accident, we attended funerals, picked up the wreckage, ran off the backlog of train traffic, cooperated with the NTSB and the various federal and state agencies, dealt with congressional investigations, and worked hard on developing a plan that would prevent this mistake from ever happening again.

All through this horrible time, I kept falling back on the principles that I had learned throughout my career and life. It was these convictions that kept me going every day through the funerals, hospital visits, union meetings, interviews, and depositions. It was then that this book was born.

WHAT THIS BOOK IS *NOT* ABOUT

In the classic *As a Man Thinketh*, James Allen (1983) said something I find truly profound when he observed, "A man cannot directly choose his circumstances, but he can choose his thoughts, and so, indirectly, yet surely, shape his circumstances." I think what Allen means is that it takes time to acquire the talents, skills, and abilities to make someone the kind of person that others willingly follow. It comes gradually, as it did for Moses.

When Moses realized his vision of freeing the Israelites from the bonds of slavery, he prematurely supposed that he could do it right away. He thought he was a leader and expected his brethren to recognize it. But they did not. It took the next forty years of Moses' life to develop the capability, adeptness, and gifts that were required to lead his people out of captivity.

So what is leadership? Is it who we are as an individual? Is it a particular quality or trait that we have? Is leadership an action we take? Are we born with leadership skills or are they acquired over time?

I have been told that there are more than 350 definitions of leadership. Over the past 25 years, I have read everything I could lay my hand's on about the subject. I have read all the classics—Drucker, Kotter, Senge, Grove, Creech, Maxwell, and others. And yet, when you ask me, "What is leadership?" I find it difficult to give a solid answer.

This confirms James MacGregor Burns's (1978) conclusion that leadership is "one of the most observed and least understood phenomena on earth." Although defining leadership can be quite a challenge—if not an impossible one—I have found that most people know it when they see it. And, conversely, when effective leadership is absent from the lives of leaders, most people would agree that the organization they are leading suffers.

In many ways, leadership is like the Abominable Snowman, whose footprints are everywhere but who is nowhere to be seen. Literally thousands of empirical investigations of leaders have been conducted in the last 75 years alone, but no clear and unequivocal understanding exists as to what distinguishes leaders from nonleaders, and perhaps more important, what distinguishes effective leaders from ineffective leaders and effective organizations from ineffective organizations.

When people talk about leadership you hear words like

- power
- influence
- leverage
- compassion
- humility
- gentleness
- generosity
- patience

Leaders are called people who "make things happen" or "don't put up with any nonsense." This is all well and good, but it still comes up short of telling us what leadership truly is.

For whatever else it may be, leadership certainly is invaluable. It is so important that it must be nourished, cultivated, and used wisely. Leadership used wisely can stir the soul of men and women to accomplish great things. It can also be used unwisely in such a way that it will lead to the frustration of a group and the eventual deterioration of an organization.

Having had a great passion for the subject of leadership for a number of years, I have come away with two one-word explanations of leadership. First, leadership is influence. Leadership cannot take place unless you are influencing the lives of others.

The second one-word explanation is "everything." As Lovett H. Weems, Jr., states,

> The best of message, opportunity, resources, facilities, and people will count for little if leadership falters and is ineffective. The task of leadership is change. Leaders inspire others to their best efforts in order to do better, to attain higher purposes. Leaders are not satisfied with the status quo. They are not satisfied with maintaining things as they are. They are idealists who believe things can be better. (Weems, 1999, p. 112)

But this book is not about leadership. Nor is this book about the differences between leadership and management. It is not about managers who do things right and leaders who do the right things. Nor is it about turning the crank well or turning the right crank. It is not about leading change in turbulent times or managing in the "E" world.

THEN WHAT IS THIS BOOK ABOUT?

At its core, this book is about what successful people have said are the salient characteristics of the best boss or bosses they have ever had and why. These characteristics are universal. They work in times of change, in times of turbulence, in good times and bad. They are seen by both the people you work for and the people who work for you.

My father was a great boss. I know because the people who worked for him told me so. My father was and still is my idol. He was a supervisor for a chemical company. It always seemed like he got the toughest assignments. He was the troubleshooter, the turn-around specialist. It always seemed like his bosses were the up-and-comers of the corporation.

We lived in a small, working-class suburb. It was impossible for us to go out to the local shopping center (before they were called malls) and not see someone who worked for my dad. It was always the same. We would meet on the sidewalk and a smile would come over the person's face upon seeing my father. The person could not wait to introduce his or her spouse and children. My dad would shake hands and then introduce them to my brother and me. After a firm handshake and concentrated eye contact, the person would always tell my brother and me, "Your dad is a great boss."

After hearing it over and over again, I started to wonder what it really meant to be a great boss. I learned a lot from the way my dad talked about his bosses. It was the regular subject of conversation around the dinner table every night. Some of them were obviously only interested in their next assignment. Others were destined for greatness. How each would do was revealed in the stories Dad would tell about them.

It was these dinner table discussions that helped me so much later on when I was in a management role, supervising people who were all older than I. Good news or bad, praise or criticism, I always projected how those people would explain my words, actions, and behavior to their families at the dinner table that evening. That is a tough audience to play to. If you play well to them, you are doing a pretty good job as a boss.

In discussions with employees over the years, I would always ask them, "Who was the best boss you ever worked for and why?" As my role and responsibilities grew, I was able to have that same conversation with managers of other Fortune 500 companies. They always seemed to come back to one of five major themes. As I remember the great ones I worked for, most of them concentrated on a single, central principle. One alone would make a person successful. The five of them together would define greatness. That is what this book is about.

WHAT I'D LIKE YOU TO GET OUT
OF READING THIS BOOK

Nearly all bosses can stand a little bit of adversity, but if you want to test a boss's character, give him or her power. Probably like you, I've seen my fair share of people who, when given the chance to be a boss, have really blown it. They became obsessed with the trappings of power—more authority, a new title, a country club membership, a special parking space, a bigger office, or whatever else—and forgot what they were supposed to be doing.

During the American Revolution, a man in civilian clothes rode past a group of soldiers repairing a small defensive barrier. Their leader was shouting instructions at them but making no other attempt to help them. Asked why by the rider, the leader said with great dignity, "Sir, I'm a sergeant!" The stranger apologized, dismounted, and proceeded to help the exhausted soldiers. The job done, he turned to the corporal and said, "If you need some more help, son, call me." With that, Commander-in-Chief George Washington remounted his horse and rode on. One man had a title . . . the other was a great boss.

By understanding the definition of a great boss, I hope you will see the big picture better and look beyond mere figures. I hope you will be less concerned with the stuff and things of your job and more concerned about the people you impact. Have more patience with those who are different from you. Focus more on the vision of your organization and less on programming it. Be less concerned with your rights and more concerned with your responsibilities.

As I think you'll see, this book is not only about business or working in an organization, it is about life. Every day we are asked to make decisions. Every day we must decide how to handle the various situations that come our way. Great bosses take the inevitable lemons of life and make lemonade. As Booker T. Washington has been credited with saying, "Character, not circumstances, makes the person."

To qualify to be a great boss, a person must not only have a certain amount of maturity to deal with life experiences, he or she must have a certain kind of character. The foundation of that character is what follows. And that character defines the great boss.

2

The Importance of Great Bosses in Today's World

Inventories can be managed, but people must be led.
—H. Ross Perot

Imagine the horror. You are the boss of a major company, and you are attending an important meeting. Your second in command is called away for a moment, then returns ashen-faced. His news: Your company's last five quarters have been a lie. Reported profits never existed, and your books have been cooked for several quarters.

This sounds eerily familiar to the recent spate of scandals and alleged fraud that has plagued corporate America recently. Actually, this scenario was written about in *Business Week* all the way back in 1993, when women's apparel manufacturer Leslie Fay Cos had outside auditors uncover a scandal threatening the very existence of the company. In Enron/WorldCom/Tyco fashion, Leslie Fay's CEO, John Pomerantz, claimed he knew nothing about the scandal—until he heard it from the auditors.

Staying with the good ol' days theme, in John Kotter's book *Leadership Factor* (1998), he tells a story of an interview he conducted with a retiring corporate executive. Kotter noted how the executive said that things used to be a whole lot easier a while ago. Back then, there were many opportunities for growth. Today, however, he complained that there is more competition and markets are much more mature. When the executive Kotter was interviewing first joined his company, he actually had monthly "allocation meetings" in his division, meetings in which it was decided which customer got which products. Can you believe that?

Today the opposite is true. As a result, Kotter observes, we need more and better bosses, people with vision and self-confidence. Without these people, there is no way we will continue to prosper. Some of our businesses, without them, won't even survive.

Over the past 100 years, the role of being a boss has dramatically changed. In the early part of the twentieth century, the style was more often paternalistic. Communication was typically top-down, with little opportunity for the grassroots to contribute. A clear distinction existed between "them" and "us," between workers and management. Employees were told what to do and were not valued as having a contribution to make to the company. It was not necessary for workers to understand their organization's vision or values.

In the last 30 years, those organizations that have been successful have leaders who recognize that their people are their greatest single asset. They have used effective communication to ensure that their people have a greater understanding of how the leader wants to grow the business, what the goals are, and how they can contribute to achieving those goals. In short, these companies have been lead by great bosses.

Organizations that have great bosses are most often successful. But successful organizations do not always have great bosses. The world is full of organizations that operate successfully from a business or financial perspective but have lousy people running them.

In the past, being a successful business was good enough. The organization survived: it made money. Today, however, factors are converging to create a new way of doing business. With this new perspective there is a fundamental shift in how we think about work and about people at work. Organizations that insist on the old mind-set are scrambling madly for good people to hire and great bosses to lead them. They lose millions of dollars through their inability to keep good people once they have hired them. Their reactive mindsets waste millions each year trying to find the simple tricks for effective recruiting and retention practices. Yet there is no quick fix.

Those attempting to explain good leadership have suggested that leadership and being a great boss are a science. From the mechanistic influence of Frederick Taylor's 1911 book *The Principles of Scientific Management* to the "humanistic, behavioral science" approaches of the 1960s, to the search for excellence and one-minute solutions of the 1980s, to the principle-centered leadership of the 1990s, people have been trying to pinpoint the answer to the question: What makes a really great boss?

While *In Search of Excellence* (Waterman & Peters, 1988) helped a lot of executives recognize the need to build a strong organizational culture, and *The One Minute Manager* (Johnson & Blanchard, 1983) reminded all managers to set goals and give praise, most managers in the 1980s found themselves looking for more. Having effective habits and the right principles are the keys, suggested Stephen Covey in *Principle Centered Leadership* (1992).

But with all respect to these classic works, they each come up short in answering our question. We viscerally know that great bosses are critical to any organization's well-being. How then can we put our finger on what a great boss really is?

Not long ago, when I was at a golf outing hosted by Price Waterhouse for leaders of several Fortune 500s, some friends and I were sitting around the clubhouse and catching up on events over the past several months. The conversation seemingly bounced all over the place, from our inflated golf scores, to Wall Street's latest announcements, to the latest gossip of who's changing companies and why.

In the midst of all the platitudes and chatter, my good friend Ralph Getz, a former vice president at UPS, brought up the recent downfall of our mutual acquaintance, Jacques Nasser, the now former CEO of Ford Motor Company. Ralph made a point that seemed to resonate among all of us seated around the table: Jacques failed to do what all great bosses must do: Give an organization somebody they can believe in.

Every time I get together with CEOs and vice presidents from some of America's finest and most successful companies, the subject of what makes a great boss always seems to come up. This has been especially true given recent events. The collapse of Enron and other huge companies like WorldCom, Tyco, and others, probably more than any other recent event in U.S. business history, has pointed a laser-sharp finger at the critical necessity of trust and respect from those who lead America's companies.

In times of turmoil, great bosses matter more than ever before. If generalizations were not so perilous, it would be tempting to infer that something is fundamentally changing with regard to what it means to be a great boss. In fact, something is. Thousands of bosses around the country—like my friend Roy Roberts, executive vice president of General Motors—have been spurred by revolt or, more often, by nose-diving sales and service and are looking to change, going beyond the old military leadership approach to one where all employees feel empowered and encouraged to be candid.

Moreover, developing great bosses may well prove to be the most strategic issue facing organizations today. A recent Wilson Learning survey of 25,000 workers at various companies found a surprising 69 percent of employee job satisfaction related to the leadership skills of their bosses. Whether or not those at the helm can learn to be great bosses may be the key to future profitability and growth. As employers can no longer guarantee employment, the days are over when a boss can make people work long hours, threaten them if they don't work, give them dirty data, or don't tell them the truth. In its place, those who manage and oversee others need to become the kind of bosses to whom employees can respond in favorable ways.

In *Top Dog*, J. David Pincus and J. Nicholas DeBonis (1994) pinpointed four workplace issues that top bosses believe are most important to employees:

1. Employees want bosses who invite them to be participants in workplace decisions.
2. Employees want bosses who share information with them openly during good and bad times.
3. Employees want bosses who are sensitive and responsive to workers' personal and professional needs.
4. Employees want a relationship with management based on partnership, not powership.

Nevertheless, they also found that employees are too often disheartened by their bosses' sluggish efforts to adapt the same policies and practices that the bosses themselves preach. It seems that bosses would rather talk about changes instead of making them. In far too many cases, marginal bosses cling to the belief that authority and control are rights they have earned through their hard work and loyalty.

GREAT BOSSES ARE *NOT* GREAT MANAGERS

John C. Maxwell in his classic *Developing the Leader Within You* (2000) contrasted the difference between mere management and being a great boss. Maxwell asserted that management is the process of assuring that the program and objectives of the organization are implemented. Being a great boss, on the other hand, has to do with casting vision.

Maxwell points out that a boss may be in control because he has been appointed to a position. In that position, he or she may have authority. But being a really great boss is more than having the technical training and following the proper procedures. Real leadership—or in other words being a really great boss—is being the person others will gladly and confidently follow.

The great boss knows the difference between being merely a manager and being someone people will get behind.

- The manager drives his workers; the great boss coaches them.
- The manager depends upon authority; the great boss depends on goodwill.
- The manager inspires fear; the great boss inspires enthusiasm.
- The manager fixes blame for the breakdown; the great boss fixes the breakdown.
- The manager knows how it is done; the great boss shows how.

At their core, people do not want to be managed. They want to be led. Whoever heard of a world manager? World leader, yes. Education leader, yes. Political leader. Religious leader. Scout leader. Community leader. Labor leader. Business leader. Yes. They lead. They do not manage. If you really want to manage something or somebody, start with managing yourself.

When the conduct of men is designed to be influenced, persuasion, kind, unassuming persuasion, should ever be adopted. It
is an old and true maxim that a drop of honey catches more flies
than a gallon of gall. So with men. If you would win a man to
your cause, first convince him that you are his true friend.
Therein is a drop of honey that catches his heart, which, say
what he will, is the great high road to his reason, and which,
once gained, you will find but little trouble in convincing his
judgment of the justice of your cause, if indeed that cause really
be a just one. On the contrary, assume to dictate to his judgment,
or to command his action . . . and he will retreat within himself,
close all the avenues to his head and his heart. . . . Such is man,
and so he must be understood by those who lead him.

                                             —Abraham Lincoln

WHAT A GREAT BOSS IS *NOT*

Here's a simple, yet immensely powerful truth—a boss's single
most important job is to provide leadership, and bosses do not
lead departments, divisions, or companies, they lead people. I
have learned over 25 years in corporate America that the extent to
which a boss is prepared to deal with this reality influences in
every possible way his or her ability to succeed and profoundly
impacts the company's ability to make a profit. But bosses are
each unique individuals with their own idiosyncrasies and nu-
ances. To begin to grasp what a great boss is may be best accomplished at first by looking at what a great boss is not.

Stephen Covey wrote a wildly successful book describing the
seven habits of highly effective people. Well, if there are habits
that people can acquire to make them effective, then there should
also be habits that bosses will want to shed that cause them to be
ineffective. Here are some I have been thinking about and working on. Bosses who want to be effective and stay on the road
toward greatness will be careful about the following.

Spending Too Much Time Managing and Not
Enough Time Leading

Warren Bennis notes that most organizations are over-
managed and underled. As I touched on earlier, there are major

differences between managing and being a great boss. Here are a few more:

- Managers think short term; great bosses think long term.
- Managers control and minimize change; great bosses initiate change.
- Managers are process-oriented (how it is done); great bosses are result-oriented (why and whether it is done).
- Managers motivate by rules and regulations; great bosses movitate by empowerment and vision.

Spending Too Much Time Being Reactive (Responding to Ideas) instead of Being Proactive (Creating Ideas)

The great boss is a proactive fire lighter, not a reactive fire fighter. Many managers spend so much time dealing with issues in a crisis mode that they have precious little time left to deal with the longer-term issues so as not be to caught behind the change curve.

Not Being in Balance

Balance is an essential, though commonly overlooked, ingredient of being a great boss. Without complementary character and behavioral traits, how else could today's bosses simultaneously fulfill the increasing number of responsibilities and roles being thrust on them each day? To fulfill those responsibilities, great bosses cannot be out of balance. They must be both active and passive. Being a great boss involves giving as well as taking, empathizing as well as directing, waiting as well as taking, giving as well as directing, waiting as well as acting.

Passive and active traits must be blended to forge a balanced great boss. The active boss tends to be viewed as someone who

- makes things happen.
- performs tasks personally.
- makes decisions unilaterally and individually.
- talks.
- orchestrates change.
- teaches.

On the other hand, the more passive boss is more often looked at as someone who

- delegates tasks to others.
- engages in participative, shared decision-making.
- listens.
- allows change to happen naturally.
- learns.
- leads through personal presence and empathy.

In reality there is no totally active or totally passive leader, only varying blends of both traits. The effectiveness of the boss is enhanced by the interplay of active and passive traits. The great boss must certainly be capable of "makings things happen" through planning, budgeting, and program implementation. He or she must also possess the patience to wait for things to happen as the result of timing or people's moods.

Likewise, the effective leader balances individual decision-making with group deliberation, personal tasks performance with delegation, and formality with informality. The well-balanced boss listens as well as talks, learns as well as teaches, and emotes as well as thinks.

Most certainly, problems inevitably erupt when a leader becomes too active or too passive. Lack of balance leads to lack of effectiveness. It is unavoidable. Overly active bosses (and their organizations) are likely to experience the following interpersonal and organizational problems:

1. Premature decision-making and action
2. Overwork and overcommitment
3. Precipitation of confrontations and conflicts
4. Poor interpersonal communication and feedback
5. Lack of rapport building with individual team members
6. Difficulty in getting people to implement decisions and programs
7. Resistance to change

The overly passive leader, on the other hand, is prone to a different set of problems:

1. Indecisive, inconsistent decision-making
2. Ineffectiveness in inspiring and motivating others

3. Wasting time in frequent meetings and informal group deliberations
4. Sloppy coordination and integration of activities and programs
5. Organizational stagnation and preoccupation with the status quo
6. Heavy dependence on team members for work progress
7. Tendency for organizational problems to escalate out of control

A careful examination of the demands of balanced bosses can prove overwhelming. While agreeing on the need for such individuals, it is easy for one boss to feel overwhelmed at the prospect of being all things to all people. Indeed, the boss who tries to be all things in all situations will probably achieve little or nothing at all. In the end, it is balance that must be the benchmark. Remember that human action can be modified to some extent, but human nature cannot be changed.

Spending Too Much Time Doing and Not Enough Time Dreaming and Planning

We have all heard the expression, "Just don't sit there, do something." At times, however, bosses need to practice, "Just don't do something, sit there." A great boss will balance out doing and dreaming, activity and quiet, energy and hibernation. A great boss will have less on the "do list" and free up time to "just sit there" and not always be chasing his own taillight in the traffic of life. Many bosses are entirely too busy with the day-to-day issues and spend comparatively little time in creative dreaming and time alone planning. Peter Drucker (1994) says that action without thinking is the cause of every failure.

Spending Too Much Time Teaching the Many and Not Enough Time Training the Few

The war will not be won from behind your desk or computer screen. Many bosses invest entirely too much time in grandiose meetings and strategy sessions despite the fact that statistics show that 70 to 80 percent of most audiences are not listening and will not apply what they are getting. Speaking to big groups needs to be balanced out with investing quality and quantity time with the few who can and will produce results.

Spending Too Much Time Doing It Themselves and Not Enough Time Doing It through Others

Bad bosses try to do it all by themselves; great bosses get others to help them. There are really only two choices in being a boss: Do it yourself, or get others to help you carry the load. Today is the day of the team and collaborative leadership, not "the Lone Ranger." I have been in the hiring position numerous times through the years, and the person I am always looking for is the one who does his or her work through people, not for people or with people. Delegate or suffocate, which will it be?

Making Too Many Decisions Based on Organizational Politics and Too Few Decisions Based on Vision and Mission

I wish we had more bosses in all segments of organizations— including government, the nonprofits, and the private sector— who do the right thing and are not overly worried about the politically correct thing. Great bosses do not hold their wet finger in the wind to see which way it is blowing, but they use that same finger to turn the pages of vision and integrity.

ARE GREAT BOSSES MADE OR BORN?

The assumption is often made that those who are great bosses are so naturally out of an inborn set of attributes, which hardly leaves a choice. In other words, much of the conventional wisdom holds that bosses are born, not made. A parallel with musical talent is often drawn—some people very early are known to be able to sing a tune, learn to play an instrument, or even compose original music with apparently very little effort. That being a great boss is a gift, like music, may be obvious, but perhaps the analogy should be pressed a little further. When it is acknowledged that a young person is gifted with musical talent, he or she is encouraged, sometimes even forced to submit to training so that the gift may be developed for the benefit of all who will listen. At first, only parents and grandparents delight to hear the fumbling, discordant attempts of the child to play the instrument. However, as the skill develops, the audience broadens. Much the same should be applied to the development of a great boss. The inborn talent may be there, but effectiveness in being a great boss waits for the development of a needed skill set.

A story was told to me years ago by a friend about a farmer who was standing alongside his field, which was now almost ready for harvest. There were long straight rows of several different kinds of vegetables: bright green carrot tops, full heads of cabbage, bright orange pumpkins, carefully propped-up tomato plants, and many rows of tall, proud stalks of corn. A neighbor happened to come by for a visit, and the farmer rather boastfully exclaimed, "Look at my beautiful field and the wonderful garden I have made." The neighbor, being a religious man, began to scold the farmer. "You should not be so boastful; after all, it was God who made that field, and you should thank Him." "Oh, I am thankful," replied the farmer, "but you should have seen this field when God had it all by Himself!"

This story adds emphasis to the idea that natural talents are in need of development. The gift we call being a great boss should be no exception. Natural-born great bosses will always have a following, but where will they lead their followers, and who will be most advantaged, the leaders or the followers? If being a great boss is a gift, who should be the recipient of that gift? Think again of the music analogy. When the musician learns to play well, he may receive some reward, if only the self-satisfaction that results from accomplishment. But the greater benefit goes to those whose lives are made more joyful and peaceful as they listen to beautiful music skillfully played. So it is with being a great boss. If the great boss leads with increasing understanding, sensitivity, communication and other leadership skills, the lives of those who follow and the organization will be greatly enhanced.

It is incumbent to give attention to the development of this important skill set. How this could be best accomplished is the subject for the remainder of this book. There should be no argument that investment in the development of bosses will pay huge dividends in every segment of society: religious, economic, industrial, and political. To raise the skill level of bosses will produce the same effect as an incoming tide. Anchored in the harbor are large luxury liners, professional fishing boats, perhaps a navy destroyer, small rowboats, and a canoe paddled by young boys. But when the tide comes in, all boats are lifted to a higher level. So too it will be with the development of those who aspire to become great bosses.

3

It All Stems from Vision

Vision is the art of seeing the invisible.
        —Jonathan Swift

Far too many people mistakenly look at business today as a short sprint rather than a long-distance race. They seem to be saying, "If you can't get it together in the next 15 minutes, you are dead in the water. Someone else will get there first, faster." Remember, however, being fast and first is all too often its own liability. There are lots of others out there, biding their time, learning from the mistakes of their competitors, and making plans to do the job even better. VisiCalc was fast and first with the computer spreadsheet. It lost out to Lotus, which lost out to Excel . . . and the company that developed VisiCalc does not even exist anymore. The fast and first PCs came from Sol, from Altair, and from a dozen other names now long-forgotten. The first portable computers came from companies like Osborne Computer (also extinct). Apple had one of the first handheld personal computers (the now ubiquitous Personal Digital Assistant), but who remembers the Newton? Today, everyone calls them "palm pilots" the way they call tissues "Kleenex." Boeing was not first in commercial aviation (remember De Haviland's Comet?) and Hewlett-Packard's Personal Computer Group took 17 years to top the PC market.

In other words, it does not really matter who gets there first, so long as you figure out a way to create a vision of real value, that you doggedly persist in expanding that value to others, and that you continually strive to enhance the vision. The five skills I discuss in the next chapters that define the truly great boss receive their direction and mandate from the vision of the organization. Enron's vision was never clear. In the middle of the firestorm following the announcement of the company's collapse, their Web site said, "It is really hard to explain what Enron does." If that was the case, should anybody have ever been surprised when the company ended up doing what they did?

At its core, the vision of an organization is what dictates

- doing the right things for the right reasons.
- where to set your expectations.
- what kind of risks to take and which mistakes to avoid.
- what kind of action plans and solutions you should take to your boss.
- how to follow up.

The very essence of being a great boss is that you have to have vision. You cannot blow an uncertain trumpet. Vision is the part of the hand that connects each of the five fingers together. A strong, well-conceived vision enables the fingers to play even the most difficult Tchaikovsky or Brahms pieces. A weak, poorly implemented vision finds it hard to bang out even "Chopsticks" or "Mary Had a Little Lamb." That is the difference between a good vision and a bad vision.

However, a bad vision looks a lot like a good vision on the surface. How many stores have you gone into in the last few months and seen a sign hanging behind the counter that said something like "We value our customers" and yet, minutes later, you found yourself ignored, treated in an unfriendly manner or worse by the staff?

Like seemingly everything else in life, it is only when we look deeper that we can finally see the real truth. And the truth is this: The ability of an organization to create, articulate, implement, reinforce, and ultimately enhance a clear vision is the supreme determinant in deciding whether the organization will succeed or fail.

To be a boss of vision in an organization with its own clear direction is frankly tough. Bosses in successful organizations are generally viewed more as implementers and people who are doing generally what they are supposed to be doing, rather than as people of vision. Nevertheless, there are great bosses in successful organizations that have their own clear and concise vision. Organizations became successful because of their great bosses.

Within the vast majority of organizations that are not distinguished and living by a clear vision, it is actually much easier to stand out as a great boss. It is more often in marginal organizations that the vision of the boss becomes paramount. In the face of a fledgling or even nonexistent vision for the organization, it follows that it is the responsibility of each boss within the organization to create his or her own vision.

The vast majority of people within an organization are more likely to follow the vision of their boss more than any other single actor, especially if the organization is not really set on a defined course. Sara Melendez in the book *The Leader of the Future* (Hesselbein et al., 1996) observes,

> The leaders I admire have a clear vision of how things should be. They are able to communicate that vision so that others can share in it, and then get others to work together as a unit, each contributing his or her best toward the achievement of that vision. In order to have a clear vision, it is necessary to see the present clearly as well. (p. 296)

In the same book, Alfred C. Decrane, Jr., says great bosses

> who can spark the imagination with a compelling vision of a worthwhile end that stretches beyond what is known today, and who can translate that to clear objectives, are the ones we follow. The Federalist Papers confirm that Madison and his colleagues understood that the most elegant documents and structures were irrelevant if they did not help the readers form a vision, an outcome, through clearly stated, overarching objectives. (p. 249)

Vision is the first step toward being a great boss. It is the envelope that contains those attributes and skills great bosses possess. The only limits are, as always, those of vision. Nothing good in life really happens unless first a dream is born. It's like the rock pile that ceases to be a rock pile the moment a single man contemplates it, bearing within him the image of a cathedral.

FINDING OUT WHAT THE VISION IS

In the vast majority of organizations, there often exists confusion over what exactly the vision is. Clearly, a major role of a boss is to lead the process that brings the organization to follow or develop a compelling vision, or both. Often vision and mission are used as synonyms, but they are not the same things. Mission is reality—the reason—the organization exists.

Vision is a picture of the future. At Burlington Northern Santa Fe Railroad, our vision is "To realize the tremendous potential of BNSF by providing transportation services that consistently meet our customer's expectations."

Vision and mission must be consistent. The organization's mission statement (what it is) flows from the vision (what it wants to be) and vice versa. Nor is vision the same as philosophy. The organization mission and the vision flow from the philosophy, the core values in which the organization is rooted. The philosophy of BNSF—our core values—are style, community, liberty, equality, and efficiency. These never change.

Unlike the organization's philosophy, a vision is not written in stone. It can and should be changed, updated, added to, and subtracted from on a regular basis. Everyone must think of it as a transitional document in order to foster an atmosphere of a growing organization and an organization in which change is the norm.

Vision is a covenant between the organization and the community of stakeholders it serves. In order to effectively lead the organization to a shared vision, the great boss must have a personal vision of what makes the organization excellent. A great boss leads the organization toward the realization of the vision. That does not mean he or she must do all the work, but he or she must be the cheerleader, encourage the designing of the strategies, oversee the implementation of the various parts of the strategic plan, and so on. This role cannot be delegated.

If the boss's personal vision and the organization's vision conflict and resolution cannot be achieved, the boss might best leave.
In fact, any staff member who cannot support the vision ought to
be encouraged to leave. The boss's role is to help focus the vision
so that the future can be seen clearly. The great boss must personally advocate the organization's vision in writing, speaking, and
living.

Boards cannot provide vision without the leadership of the
organization's bosses. This is true for several reasons. Board
members can be on the board for only a few years. Board members
are very part-time, and their role is to be the trustees of the
mission and vision, not leaders of the vision's development.
Board members understand neither the everyday workings of the
organization nor how to professionally do what the organization
does. That is the role of the professional staff. Board members
have a limited ability to articulate a perspective on how to do it,
although the boards help bring reality to the vision by helping
define strategies.

Great bosses need not be charismatic visionaries to lead the
vision. They need only a clear understanding of their role, a clear
vision of their own for the organization, and the ability to articulate the organization's vision. The goal of a vision is to enhance
the viability of the organization and to align it with the philosophy and mission.

THE TWO LEVELS OF VISION

Vision has two levels. The macro-vision is for the entire organization. It includes what you want the outputs to look like, how
you want the organization to serve the stakeholders, the perspective from which you will do the mission, and the methodology.
The micro-vision is for individual programs and departments—
technology, sales, human resources, and so on.

The vision or portions of the vision can come from a staff
member, a board member, the staff, the board, a customer, a
supplier, focus groups, roundtable meetings, etc. The savvy, ex-
perienced boss recognizes good new pieces of the vision and
leads the organization toward molding those parts into the
macro-vision.

A well-articulated vision empowers everyone in the organization to understand how their actions fit into the big picture. A well-written strategic plan, the road map to vision, gives people confidence that what they are doing is consistent with the vision. It takes time to promote a vision, lead the process of vision creation, hone the vision, articulate the vision, and do all the other things a boss ought to do with, to, and for the vision.

A vision cannot be ignored and still make a difference. Groups within the organization must be assigned to develop goals and strategies to accomplish portions of the vision. These groups must also assess the effectiveness of the plan to meet the vision. The boss's role is to lead the development of the strategic plan and with the board hold those working on it accountable.

A well-articulated vision enables organizations to implement successful programs and strategies. Such a vision captures people's attention and inspires them to contribute in a number of ways. A great boss empowers others to solve problems and discover their own answers. Great bosses help their people to form a personal vision consistent with the organization's vision.

FORMING A VISION

A vision that does not lead to some kind of action is unlikely to be of much help to anybody. It goes without saying that the most important characteristic of visionary leadership is that it leads to action. Yet, turning a vision into reality can be extremely difficult.

In most cases, two distinctive types of bosses emerge when forming a vision either at the macro or micro level. The first type, authoritarian, results in "people pleasing" rather than on the philosophy and mission of the organization. The follower focuses his or her attention on the leader and himself or herself. Pleasing the boss, rather than forming a vision, becomes the goal.

The second, and unfortunately less popular, type of vision formation involves bosses who actually know where they are going. Bill Walsh, the former head coach of the San Francisco 49ers, was thought eccentric because of how extensively he planned his plays in advance of each game. Most coaches would wait to see how the game unfolded, then respond with plays that seemed appropriate. Not Bill Walsh.

Walsh would pace the sidelines with a big sheet of plays that his team was going to run, no matter what. He wanted the game to respond to him. Walsh won three Super Bowls with his "eccentric" proactive approach. But all he did was to act on the crucial difference between creating and responding. He compiled a .617 winning percentage with a 102-63-1 career record that included 10 wins in 14 postseason games. He was a coach who looked into the future.

Being a great boss not only requires thinking about where the organization needs to go but also looking at how it will get there. We look ahead so that we won't get behind. Only by seeing the invisible can we attempt the impossible. The critical need of looking ahead is the process of creating your organizational future before it happens. Like Bill Walsh, it is creating your own actions in advance so that your life will respond to you. It is attempting to write history in advance.

Looking ahead gives direction. It's like using a highlighter on a road map that indicates where you are, where you are going, and how you are going to get there. It indicates present location, proposed destination, and a planned route for reaching the desired outcome.

This road map not only provides information for where you are going; it also suggests where you are not going. Planned abandonment—what you must not do—is just as important as planned adventure—what you will do. Organizations do not have the time, resources, and personnel to do everything. So looking ahead helps one determine the few things that are worth doing, and worth doing well.

One of the best benefits of creatively looking ahead is that it allows you to simplify. It allows you to repack your bags, lighten your load, take only what is needed for your journey. Looking ahead helps you to create rather than react. Looking ahead allows you the opportunity to create your own actions in advance so that life will respond to you. At all times in your life you are either creating or reacting.

CREATION VERSUS REACTION

"Creation" and "reaction" have the same letters in them, exactly. They are anagrams. Each step along our journey we are faced with a choice either to create or to react. Many bosses spend their entire days reacting. Like goalies in a hockey game, with pucks flying at them all day, they react. We react to news, cars in traffic, people, events, challenges, and obstacles. But there's a better way to live. It involves making choices and following plans. It involves choosing to create. We create by planning, forecasting, and looking ahead. As John Rockefeller said, "Business is nothing more than the art of forecasting" (Abels, 1965, p. 190).

Great bosses grasp that looking ahead saves time. I have written in my day planner: "One hour of planning saves three hours of execution." I am a proponent of looking ahead for its time savings return. It provides me with a marvelous return on my investment. I only have 24 hours in a day and 365 days in a year. If I do not use them wisely by looking ahead, I will forever forfeit those opportunities.

Great bosses also realize that looking ahead allows them to build on their strengths. Effective leaders determine what the organization can do best, and then they do it. When the organization is expanded, it is expanded building on strengths, not on weaknesses. The best resources—time, money, and personnel—are assigned to the opportunities that build on the strengths.

Great bosses recognize that looking ahead reduces crisis. As we live our daily lives, the two controlling influences will be either our plans or our pressures. When we look ahead and choose to plan, we take charge and control of our days. If we fail to look ahead, we will spend our days in crisis mode. We will fall into a trap of "panic planning." And contrary to public opinion, no one works well under pressure for long.

Great bosses comprehend that looking ahead gives energy. Failing to plan is like diffused light—no energy, no power; whereas planning is like light focused—great power, great energy. Unfocused sunlight will warm your body. But focus that same sunlight through a magnifying glass and it will set a leaf on fire. Take that same light and intensify its focus, and it becomes a laser beam that can cut through steel. Failing to focus—not having a vision—dissipates our energy on less important matters, improper agendas, and lost crusades. We become dabblers, wasting our power on the trivial many. Much activity exists, but little productivity. On the other hand, when our look is focused, concentrated on the vital few, we are renewed, revitalized, and remade.

THE STRATEGIC NATURE OF A VISION

Bosses who think strategically are able to picture a range of possibilities several stages ahead of the current phase of organizational development. Like a good chess player, it was said of Napoleon that he could envisage several steps ahead, with the various permutations of competitive response.

Great bosses are pragmatic rather than "head in the clouds." The vision developed will lead to strategies and tactics, which they will need to engage with, and succeed in, the real world. These strategies must therefore be based on a realistic appraisal of the environment in which the organization finds itself, the resources at its disposal, and the opportunities that exist.

Great bosses have an innate understanding of timing. They have the patience to wait until the timing is right to make a major intervention, yet they have the boldness to strike decisively when the moment is right. They, and their organizations, are alert and ready to seize an opportunity.

Bosses whose current work is future focused are more likely to be working strategically: investing their time in developing people and their capabilities for the future of the organization as well as managing the current needs of the organization. A great boss is willing to work with others in alliances and agreements to make a more significant intervention than either party would be able to make alone. If necessary, the great boss is willing to subjugate the organization's need for recognition to making progress against a broader agenda for change.

READING THE COMPASS CORRECTLY

Almost every time the word boss is mentioned, in what direction do people instinctively think? South. Say the word boss and most minds migrate to the people who are under their care. At leadership conferences, people generally think, "I'm going to learn how to improve my ability to lead the people I have entrusted to me." South. It's the typical boss's first instinct.

But many people do not realize that to be a great boss, you need to be able to lead in all directions—north, south, east and west. For example, great bosses have to lead north—those who are over them. They cannot just focus on those entrusted to their care. Through relationship and influence great bosses lead the people over them.

Great bosses also learn how to lead east and west, laterally, in peer group settings. If you don't learn how to lead laterally, if you don't know how to create win-win situations with colleagues, the whole culture can deteriorate.

So a boss must lead down, up, and laterally. But perhaps the most overlooked leadership challenge is the one in the middle. Who is your toughest leadership challenge? Yourself.

In this critical moment the aware boss realizes a foundational truth: He has to lead himself before he can lead anybody else. Unless he is squared away internally he has nothing to offer his team. This is the importance of self-leadership. And although self-leadership is not talked about much, make no mistake, it is a good part of the ballgame. How effectively can any of us lead others if our spirits are sagging, our courage is wavering, and our vision or commitment is weak?

In a recent article Daniel Goleman, the author of the best-selling book *Emotional Intelligence* (1997), analyzes why some leaders develop to their fullest potential and why most hit a plateau far from their full potential.

His conclusion? The difference is (you guessed it) self-leadership. He calls it "emotional self-control" (Goleman, 1997).

What characterizes maximized leadership potential, according to Goleman, is tenaciously staying in leadership despite overwhelming opposition or discouragement, staying in the leadership game and maintaining sober-mindedness during times of crisis; keeping ego at bay; staying focused on the mission instead of being distracted by someone else's agenda. All these indicate high levels of emotional self-control. Goleman says, "Exceptional leaders distinguish themselves because of superior self-leadership."

This is the essence self-leadership. Nobody—and I mean nobody—can do this work for you. You have to do this work yourself. Self-leadership is tough work—so tough, Dee Hock (2000) says, that most leaders avoid it. Instead, we would rather try to inspire or control our people than to do the rigorous work of reflection.

The next five chapters detail the critical skills that each great boss possesses. As you'll see, the acquisition and implementation of that skill set rests squarely on the shoulders of the boss. There is no one who can be blamed if things do not work out. And, if they do, success is all your own.

4

Do the Right Thing for the Right Reasons

The supreme quality for leadership is unquestionably integrity. Without it, no real success is possible, no matter whether it is on a section gang, a football field, in an army, or in an office.

—Dwight David Eisenhower

In a recent cartoon in the *New Yorker*, two clean-shaven middle-aged men are sitting together in a jail cell. One inmate turns to the other and says: "All along I thought our level of corruption fell well within the community standards."

A Jeff Danziger cartoon shows a boss announcing to his staff, "Gentlemen, this year the trick is honesty." From one side of the conference table, a vice president gasps, "Brilliant!" Across the table, another VP mutters, "But so risky."

Being a great boss requires moral authority. Followers have to see enough integrity in the boss's life that high levels of trust can be built. When surveys are taken about what it is that inspires a follower to throw his or her lot in with a particular leader over a long period of time, near the top of every list is integrity.

A great boss does not have to be the sharpest pencil in the drawer or the one with the most charisma. But teammates will not follow a boss with character incongruities for very long. Every time you compromise character, you compromise the ability to lead.

Some time ago we had a staff member who was struggling in his role as a boss. I started poking around a little bit. "What's going on here?" I asked.

Then the real picture emerged. One person said, "For one thing, he sets meetings and then he doesn't even show. He rarely returns phone calls and often we don't know where he is."

I spoke to that boss and said, "Let's get it straight. When you give your word that you're going to be at a certain place at a certain time and you don't show up, that's a character issue. That erodes trust in followers. You clean that up, or we'll have to move you out." If character issues are compromised, it hurts the whole team and eventually impacts mission achievement.

At the end of the day, it's the boss's job to grow in character. No one can do that work except the boss. Great bosses do that work very well.

INTEGRITY AND CULTURE

During Senate testimony in the summer of 2002, Federal Reserve Chairman Alan Greenspan spoke of an "infectious greed" that had gripped much of America's business leaders. Such greed ultimately pushed companies like Enron, Global Crossing, and WorldCom into bankruptcy. Infections or cures for the same spread through an organization's culture—meaning the set of rites and rituals, symbols, and signals that give it its unique culture. Whether good or bad, the transmitters of culture are the bosses who work within a given organization.

Culture is ordinary. Every organization has its own shape, its own aims, and its own intentions. The making of an organization is identifying those common aims and intentions and growing these into a dynamic, organic entity under the pressures of experience, contact, and discovery. The degree of success an organization ultimately attains is predicated more than any other factor upon how well the bosses shape the culture. Great bosses will impact an organization's culture in tremendous and positive ways. A marginal boss or poor boss will do the opposite. Bosses who do the right thing for the right reasons lay the foundation for a culture of real value and a long-lasting place in the minds of the organization's stakeholders.

DO THE RIGHT THING FOR THE RIGHT REASONS

Warren Buffett said it correctly when he observed that to clean up their acts, bosses don't need independent directors, oversight committees, or auditors absolutely free of conflicts of interest. They should quit talking about some bad apples and reflect instead on their own behavior. They simply need to do what's right. To better understand doing the right thing for the right reasons, we need to look deeper at what it really means.

Do

Over recent months, there have most certainly been a rising number of heated debates in business class about the subject of bosses. Not surprisingly, most discussions between seatmates turn negative almost after the first couple of sentences. Then, as the number of participants in the conversation begins to increase, the criticism for bosses does as well. However, the entire context of the conversation suddenly changes when somebody muses, "Well, at least my boss can make a decision."

It never ceases to amaze how when a boss makes a decision—whether it is a good one, a marginal one, or a determination of even terrible impact—the respect level for that same boss goes way up. For merely possessing the attribute and ability to make a decision, the esteem of that boss rises in the eyes of those around him or her.

It's what we do that counts. Not what we don't do. Taking action and making decisions are an open window into what we are about as people and as leaders. Making decisions defines our value and benchmarks our credibility.

The Right Thing

What really matters? What is central rather than peripheral? What is kernel rather than shell? What is primary rather than secondary? What is substance rather than mere form? What is essential rather than optional? What really matters?

Most bosses when asked this question—and its variations—confess that too much of their time is taken up by things that are not very important. Still, despite this, they too often have established routines that give their organization a sense of stability and security. But the vitality that comes from keeping the most meaningful things central is missing. They fail to see what the right thing is.

For the Right Reasons

There are too many bosses who think that the only thing that is right is to get by, and the only thing that is wrong is to get caught. Real character as a great boss and doing the right thing are often best observed when nobody is looking. The truth of the matter is that you almost always know the right thing to do. It's what your grandmother taught you. It's in your bones. Unfortunately, for many bosses, the hard part is in the doing.

In any moment of decision, the best thing you can do is the right thing. The worst thing you can do is nothing. This comes back to the critical aspect of making a decision. That confidence in making decisions for the great boss comes not from always being right but from not fearing to be wrong.

Joshua Lawrence Chamberlain: A Case Study in Doing the Right Thing

The hero of Little Round Top at the Battle of Gettysburg, Joshua Lawrence Chamberlain, brought to life the principle of doing the right thing for the right reasons. Chamberlain's experiences revealed his intense, often passionate feelings for his country and the men who served under him. But his empathy did not end with those who fought with him. He also showed real compassion and sensitivity to the Confederate soldiers who had opposed him. The qualities and values he held were esteemed far above many of his contemporaries. These same virtues commanded tremendous respect from his men, making Chamberlain one of the finest officers ever to serve in the United States Army.

Ulysses S. Grant, in his admiration for Chamberlain, designated him to receive the flag of surrender at Appomattox Courthouse, April 12, 1865. He was chosen to receive the formal surrender of arms and colors of the Confederate Army. At that time he rendered one of the most memorable and gallant acts of the war by giving a final salute to the soldiers of the Confederacy as they laid down their arms. Why? Because it was the right thing to do.

In looking at character and the ability to do the right thing for the right reasons, Chamberlain (1994) described his soldiers as they faced down a numerically superior enemy on Little Round Top.

> It was the force of character you had formed in the silent and peaceful years by the mother's knee and the father's side, which stood you in such stead in the day of trial. We know not of the future, and cannot plan much for it. But we can hold our spirits and our bodies sure and high. We may cherish such thoughts and such ideals, that we can determine and know what manner of men we will be whenever and wherever the hour strikes that calls us into noble action. (p. 175)

THE PILLARS OF DOING THE RIGHT THING FOR THE RIGHT REASONS

From my perspective, doing the right thing for the right reasons is founded in the pillars of consistency: credibility, reputation, risk, and accountability. These factors, more than any other, serve as the inputs of doing the right thing. When directed in the proper manner, they inevitably lead to an outcome of the right decision, at the right time, at the right place, and in the right way.

Bulletproof Consistency

The Latin root of the word *integrity* is similar to that for integer, meaning whole number. The concept of wholeness, or consistency, is clearly relevant. For now, we shall take "behavior and decisions that are consistently in line with our principles" as our working definition of acting with integrity. The dictionary would also suggest that these principles should generally be accepted as ethical and honest. One of the important elements of integrity is consistency. If we are unpredictable, if our decisions are dependent upon the day of the week and the way we are feeling, others are unlikely to see us as maintaining integrity.

After several different positions over the first five years of my career, I found myself in charge of a large division operation in Little Rock, Arkansas. This was in the early 1980s before the days of many of the buzzwords that exist today to describe bosses. I was called a manager. I got things done. I made decisions. However, what I did was, for the most part, based on pre-established guidelines emanating from policies, operating rules, and instructions. In reality, I was more of an administrator of set policies.

I worried a lot about consistency. I battled every day with thoughts like "If I allow this exception, it will weaken my power." "If I do it for one, I will have to do it for everyone." "I must be consistent, and that means doing it by the book."

One night, I was in the office working late. Most of the staff had gone home. There was a knock at my door and two employees asked if they could come in. They were two burly, seasoned railroad workers who sat down on the edge of their seats. Although I do not remember what they asked me, I have always remembered how the conversation started out. The first began by saying, "Mr. Dealy, we came here tonight to ask you to listen to us about a problem we have. We know that most supervisors would say that our company has a policy for this and it clearly defines what we must do." Then the second one took over saying, "In this case, the policy is very clear on how our situation should be handled. In fact, if it were anyone other than you, we would have given up long ago, but we believe that our situation is a little bit different and deserves special consideration."

What they said after that still sticks with me as though it was yesterday. "We have been watching what you do and how you do it. We have always believed that you would always do the right thing for the right reasons." Then they asked their question.

That was a defining moment in my life. I thought, "They were watching me? They trusted me? They believed that I would do the right thing for the right reasons? What should I do?"

As it unfolded, I do not even remember whether I granted their request, whatever it was. I do remember, however, having the unquestionable and unconditional feeling that they trusted me and they would continue to trust me, regardless of the outcome of my decision. I was in awe of that situation and their trust. From that point on in my career, I was determined to examine what it was that I did to earn their trust and respect and how to lead and manage in ways that continued to develop that type of credibility.

After 26 years in business, for even the best of rules, instructions, and policies, I have found that there are always exceptional situations that lie outside their original intent. Dishearteningly, however, I have seen many a manager forcing these situations into a box like a square peg in a round hole. They work hard to make it either black or white because then the decision is easy. But, forcing things to be black or white does not build credibility. Recognizing when they are gray and reacting accordingly does.

Rob Krebs, Chairman, CEO and President of the Santa Fe Railway and then the BNSF Railway, a man I have had the pleasure of working for since 1993, always says, "Consistency is the hobgoblin of the simple mind."

The most important word in this chapter's title is "Do." It's what we do that counts, not what we don't do. Taking action and making decisions are an open window into what we are about. They define our values and our character, and they define whether or not we're truly a great boss.

Established Credibility

Doing is the first step toward establishing credibility. Without credibility, a boss is nothing—general with no troops, a coach with no players, a pastor with no warm bodies in the pews. In addition, a leader with no followers is not recognized by his or her boss as a person who gets things done.

Our decisions are portals into our true selves. They define our values. They give the people around us insights into our value system. People watch whether and how we make decisions.

For me, doing the right thing for the right reasons has required constant vigilance throughout my career. As a young supervisor, I was actually trained on how *not* to establish credibility. It wasn't even a consideration. Status and the bogus credibility that supposedly came with it were derived through superfluous things like office size, whether there was a reserved parking space or not, and the number of meetings one sat in on.

I was never told the importance of credibility as a part of my performance evaluations. My bosses instructed me through their actions that the needless was really all that mattered. I was a boss because the title bestowed that on me. Nothing more, nothing less. Isn't that the way too many bosses are today—mere titleholders with a cool title on their office door?

Credibility is earned. It is the antithesis of a title or a good-looking business card. Credibility is accumulated over time through an open, honest process that produces relevant results. Without credibility, no one will ever take you seriously—regardless of what the name on the door may say. People will not participate in what you are trying to do, or they may even attempt to sabotage your undertaking. Credibility for a great boss means that the people around you

- take your word at face value.
- recognize your role in the decision-making process.
- believe that you will do what you say you will do.
- understand how you got your data.
- trust you to analyze the data objectively.

To build credibility, a great boss involves others in finding the necessary answers to the most important questions.

A great boss is also willing to consider all questions, whether on the surface they appear pertinent or not.

A great boss is also an equal opportunity data handler. That is, great bosses share information with everyone who needs access to that information. They do not use information as a weapon of control and power. They do not limit information access unless it is absolutely necessary. At the very least, they explain what is confidential and why.

A great boss serves as the most complete and reliable source of information—especially bad news! People automatically assume the worst—an assumption nearly impossible to dislodge. Great bosses tell people quickly when things change. Openly discussing issues and problems will defuse speculation about myth-truths and will enhance trust and credibility.

Built Reputations

Many suppose that their organization's hard assets like machinery, inventory, or technology give them the ultimate edge over their competitors. Others say it is their firm's vast financial resources that keep them on top. Although each of these is critical to an organization's ultimate success, its reputation is the most important asset. People buy your products and services, sell you theirs, and seek to develop relationships with you based primarily upon how they perceive your organization. Your reputation provides the foundation to that perception. To be blunt, you must do everything you can to preserve and enhance the reputation your company has with its customers, suppliers, strategic alliance partners, employees, and the public at large.

Great bosses realize that their and the organization's meaningful and valuable reputation begins with one fundamental factor: choices. The degree of success of a boss will be shaped dramatically by the strength of their commitment to doing the right thing all the time. Every day a boss is confronted with a myriad of choice. Some of the options will be the correct choice, others will not. By making the right choices, the boss and the organization will receive the payoffs associated with reputations of honesty, integrity, quality, and caring in everything they do. Make the wrong choices, and the boss and the organization will be plagued with mistakes, ongoing problems, unavoidable disasters, irreparable damage to reputation, and quite possibly, even their ultimate demise.

Perhaps the real tragedy of poor choices is the mental anguish, pain, and constant scrutiny that emerge from a ruined reputation. Reputation, at its core, can be defined as all that is generally believed about one's character, respectability, credit, integrity, or notoriety. Reputation is what the boss's image, performance history, and track record mean in people's minds.

A good reputation is the building and sustaining of a boss's name. Henry Ford said it right when he observed, "You can't build a reputation on what you are going to do" (1988, p. 216). By paying attention to what you are doing, you will be able to construct and maintain a strong perception of you and your organization.

Rooted Principles

When confronted with a challenging situation, the first step undertaken by the great bosses is to determine what their principles are. This may not be as easy as it sounds, particularly when faced with a difficult decision! There may be a solution that meets all of the principles. It may even be a good one! However, the chances are that there is no easy solution that comfortably fits all of your principles. Consider your leadership: Would you consider yourself to be exercising situation-based leadership or principle-based leadership? (Are your decisions based on what is expedient for the current situation, or are they based on principles?)

Ascertained Risk

Decision making—real decision-making—implies taking some measure of risk. Determining the right thing to do and the right reasons to do it often requires knowledge and decision-making ability. It involves risk-taking. Categorizing issues into black or white and then applying a set table of decision rules is not true decision-making. People might as well have an ATM machine as a boss. Again, it comes back to the closed-minded approach of consistency for consistency's sake.

I had a basketball coach my sophomore year in high school. After all these years, I can still remember the speeches he made to the team in preparation for the season. He said that we were going to be a team that took advantage of shooting 80 percent shots. At first, the players did not quite understand what he was talking about.

Just prior to the first game, after the cuts had been made, the coach sat down with each player and showed him the results of his practices that had revealed where 80 percent of his shots came from. It was obvious that the coach had done his homework and that he knew mathematically what each of his players was capable of.

Penalties for attempting to exceed one's defined capabilities during game conditions, such as trying a hook shot from the half-court line, were severe. The time to test capabilities was in practice. After the next practice following a game, those players attempting shots outside their 80 percent range were running laps around the gym . . . long after the rest of the team had showered and headed for home. They were not alone, for the players who had a shot within their 80 percent range and elected not had to take it were also running. The team went undefeated for the season. The coach's lesson was simple: In basketball, just as in life, taking unreasonable risk never was as profitable as working toward an ascertained outcome. Moreover, always waiting for the sure thing will never drive continuous success.

Simply stated, ascertained risk is manageable risk. Without question, there are certain undeniable risks that come with doing business in today's always-changing marketplace. Notwithstanding this truth, there are proven ways in which to minimize the level of risk and make it palatable to your and your organization's appetites.

Real Accountability

Many people do not know what accountability means. To give you an answer using *Webster's Dictionary*, accountability means "an obligation or willingness to accept responsibility or to account for one's actions." At its core, accountability is really the responsibility to act. However, confusing accountability with responsibility obscures the obligation to act.

At the end of the day, it is critical to understand that people count, not intangible things like "corporations" and "governments." For bosses, reciprocal accountability is the obligation of people in senior posts in organizations to answer to members of the organization for what they intend and what they contribute.

For every important responsibility there is accountability. Accountability is the obligation to answer for the discharge of responsibilities that affect others in important ways. The answering is for intentions as well as results. Whenever a boss has an important responsibility, he or she has an obligation to answer to stakeholders for decision made.

Managers have, for quite some time, been held accountable for results. These results are usually included in a manager's scorecard. In most businesses, the manager lives and dies by the numbers on the scorecard. For many of these numbers, there are trade-offs that have to or should be made for the good and betterment of the manager's own department or the good of the company. We have seen many managers deal away their credibility because they manage according to their numbers at all cost, even when it is obvious that the decision is detrimental to the greater good.

I have had peer managers publicly state that they know that the right thing to do is X, but they're going to do Y because of their numbers. They are worried about their boss. They are obviously not worried about their employees, who can see this very clearly. How can employees respect this boss? They really cannot.

General Electric under the leadership of Jack Welch was famous for the scorecard approach. This was the fundamental underpinning for their ranking system that identified the "bottom 10%." I once spoke to Bob Nardell, now CEO of The Home Depot, former GE executive, about this system during dinner and cocktail party talk. Although GE was obviously keen on accountability, decisions made to suboptimize in favor of one's own number were not tolerated. A good manager knows when it is time to take one for the team. A good manager also knows and values the credibility that gives with employees.

SOME GUIDELINES FOR ALWAYS DOING THE RIGHT THING FOR THE RIGHT REASONS

As so often happens, a boss's and an organization's reputation dies not from someone else's hand but from a self-inflicted wound. In today's news-obsessed world, no business is immune from public scrutiny. A failure to recognize this reality can lead to tragic consequences.

The ultimate decision of how to conduct oneself in the marketplace is up to each organization and the people who lead it. To help set some parameters, we've included the following guidelines to help leaders better evaluate the impact of ethical decisions on their company's reputation and their own.

1. Would any of your company's key stakeholders (employees, shareholders, upper management, strategic suppliers, or customers) be embarrassed if he or she found out about this behavior?
2. Would any of your company's key stakeholders immediately disapprove of this behavior?
3. Would any of your company's key stakeholders feel that this behavior is unusual?

4. Would any of your company's key stakeholders be upset if this activity or behavior happened to them?
5. Are decision makers concerned about the possible consequences of this behavior? Is there active or ongoing discussion about the ramifications of the behavior?
6. Would your customers be upset if this behavior or activity were publicized in a newspaper or Internet article?
7. Would this behavior spill over into other aspects of the business and negatively impact your corporate culture?
8. Would your customers jump ship if this behavior were made public?

And, if these guidelines do not give you enough of an idea, ask yourself this last question: Is this something I would do in front of my children?

5

Set Your Expectations Higher Than Your Boss's Expectations for You

> High expectations are the key to everything.
> —Sam Walton

I work in a business that runs 24/7. We have the luxury of evaluating ourselves every morning. We always tend to focus on the areas of opportunity, otherwise known as mistakes or miscues. It is very easy in any position of leadership to fall into the trap of worrying more about what our boss thinks about our performance than how we measure up to our own standards of performance. When you wake up every morning in the "how am I going to explain this to my boss" syndrome, life is not pleasant. The worst part is, your people see right through this. Instead of being a leader, you are a mouthpiece or a puppet for your boss.

I am convinced that this is one of the major drivers in credibility. People want to have a leader who is confident. One cannot exude confidence if one worries about someone else's expectations.

There have been so many times that I have heard bosses say, "Don't do that again because I'll catch hell from my boss!" The best bosses were those who led and managed so that you never saw any evidence that they even had a boss. They were their own boss. They worried about their own high, exacting standards and expectations. They were concern and even upset if the results were not acceptable, not because of what their boss would think, but because of what they felt. Those leaders gained the respect of their employees. The ones who wore their boss on their sleeve did not.

Bosses who do not have high expectations and who bounce back and forth based on their boss's reactions are unpredictable. This makes them very difficult to work for. They have great difficulty in making decisions. All of us have had a boss like this or we know someone who has. Working for these types of bosses makes us feel sorry for them. Sympathy does not, however, create respect and credibility.

Harry S. Truman had a motto displayed on his presidential desk: "The Buck Stops Here." Good bosses lead that same way. Those are real bosses. Giving people a little more than they expect is a good way to get back more than you would expect.

United Parcel Service is full of these types of managers. Before he joined GM, it was common to hear Ralph Getz talk about the real leaders he worked for at UPS because of their standards and expectations. The package business is a tough one. The on-time delivery requirements, the union work rules, the constant pressure and intensity for customer satisfaction—UPS runs a tight ship. It would be easy in that type of environment to take the easy way out and blame the bad news on the boss. That is not the way it works there.

Probably most of us have had a boss at one time or another who had to pass bad news by blaming the higher-ups. "I didn't want to make these cuts but headquarters made me." "I wanted to give you a higher annual performance evaluation, but my boss made me lower it." "I know that no one wants to work forced overtime, but you know what corporate would say if we didn't get this shipment out." Good bosses must have high standards and expectations. Good bosses have to be able to tell the truth, most importantly when the truth may be bad news.

In our company, our field general managers pride themselves in saying to their people, "Don't look any further up the ladder than me. I am headquarters as far as you are concerned. I have ownership in the decision-making process and I hold myself accountable for the outcomes. I am headquarters."

"Water-cooler talk"—like "I heard his boss made him do it"—is not complimentary to a real boss. With a real boss, you never know what his or her boss said. You don't even care. Bosses who set high expectations are known to their people as "take charge" leaders. They breed integrity and credibility. And they are great.

As Wayne Gretzky used to say, "I skate to where the puck is going to be, not where it is."

WHAT ARE EXPECTATIONS?

Among the most powerful forces we experience in life are expectations. Some expectations come from other people. Parents, spouses, peers, bosses, friends, children, neighbors, customers, and plenty of others all have their expectations of us. They expect certain things regarding our speech, our behavior, and our character. Often, the most influential expectations are the ones that go unstated. And the source of some expectations may be hard to define. We allow our lives to be determined by a powerful yet indefinite group we call "they." "They" expect this or that of me, and I feel compelled to satisfy them.

Other expectations come more clearly from within us. We accept certain norms, and expect to follow them. We prize certain goals, and expect to realize them. These internal expectations make their presence known. When they conflict with each other, then we feel the pain of division and confusion until we choose between them.

Some expectations are unjust, whether they come from inside or outside. They demand that we do what we cannot or should not do. What they ask exceeds our ability or does violence to our identity. There are other expectations that are just. They call on us to do what we can or what we need to do. They show us our responsibility to others. They contribute to the establishment of our true identity.

Expectations seem intricately tied to what philosophers have called "virtue." One general and traditional definition of virtue is "a habit that enables one to do something good easily." This very general definition is encapsulated in the old saying "Practice makes perfect." Practice over time creates a habit, an abiding ability, and a skill that enables us to do something with ease. If I pick up a knife and a piece of wood and try to carve something, or even just try to whittle the wood, I will gouge it and ruin it quickly, because I have no practice in carving wood. I have not practiced whittling or carving, and I have no ability or skill.

If, however, I spent hours a day learning to whittle or carve, I might well become skilled. I would have acquired the virtue of a carver. So too with piano playing or speaking French or dealing with customer service. Of course some people seem to have a natural ability or inclination toward various activities of soul, mind, or body. There are natural athletes, people with seemingly innate musicality or intellectual genius or a gift for languages. But without denying innate dispositions, most activities can be cultivated by practice and habit so that we can acquire the virtue to perform them more easily than we would if we did not practice.

Usually, however, we use the word virtue in everyday speech in a different sense. Virtue usually implies a moral quality. We may begin with our general definition of virtue (a habit that enables one to do something well with ease), and then apply it to moral matters in recognition of this everyday sense of the word. A moral virtue is a habit of soul that enables one to do moral good and to avoid wrong easily in some respect. For instance, the virtue of honesty in money matters means a habit of respecting the property of others, which makes it easy for me to return money belonging to someone else that I have found or easy for me not to surrender to a temptation to steal. In this case we have taken the general idea of a virtue and applied it specifically to a moral matter, to doing moral good and avoiding evil.

The matter of habit, of acquiring a skill or ability or tendency through repetition or custom or gradual development or practice, remains. Virtue at its core is a true understanding of oneself and one's abilities when setting expectations. It's a funny thing about life: If you refuse to accept anything but the best, you very often get it. The world is full of abundance and opportunity, but far too many people come to the fountain of life with a sieve instead of a tank car, a teaspoon instead of a steam shovel. They expect little, and as a result they get little.

SEEING THE EXPECTATIONS BEFORE
THEY MATERIALIZE

For a great boss, the future belongs to those who see possibilities before they become obvious. There are risks and costs to a program of action and to setting your expectations higher than those of the individuals around you. But they are far less than the long-range risks and costs of comfortable inaction. Great bosses are those who get up and look for circumstances they want, and if they cannot find them, they make them.

This is done through the development of habits. Since the time of Aristotle at least, writers interested in moral matters have noted the importance of habit in developing character and setting one's expectations. That is, they note the importance of developing habits that dispose children, and then adults, to expect to do the right thing. Custom becomes second nature. Habits incline us one way or the other. These habitual inclinations, if they dispose us toward doing good, are virtues. If they dispose us toward doing evil, they are vices.

A virtue does not destroy free will. A truthful person, for instance, is someone who is accustomed to telling the truth, even when doing so is embarrassing or personally costly. This benchmarks their expectation of themselves when it comes to truthfulness. Such a person, however, may be tempted to lie and may actually do so. The virtue of truthfulness makes it easier for the person to resist the temptation; at least if he tells a lie, it will be against his inclination and will probably prick his conscience. Virtues and vices are habits and dispositions, which make something easier or harder but not inevitable.

The sum of our habits of soul, our virtues and vices, is our character. The idea that character and virtue, which determine our expectations, are essentially private and not of concern in a setting like business is shortsighted and dangerous in the extreme. Tyco, Enron, Adelphia, Global Crossing, and the like show us what omitting character and virtue and having no valid expectations except greed can do.

GETTING WHAT YOU EXPECT AS A BOSS

You often get what you expect. As a boss, this is a very powerful reality that you can harness to work for you, or you can let it control performance in a negative way. It is your job to set and use expectations in a manner that supports and enhances performance. The theory that expectations affect performance is known as the Pygmalion Principle. Its name is derived from a Greek myth in which a sculptor named Pygmalion sculpted a statue of a woman and fell in love with it.

His love was so strong that Aphrodite transformed the statue into a real woman in answer to Pygmalion's desire. It is this transformative effect resulting from expectations that is the basis of the Pygmalion Principle. Research in the field of education has supported the theory by demonstrating that students whom the teacher believed to be smarter than the rest of the group (when they were actually randomly chosen) performed substantially better than those believed to be "average." In these experiments, the only difference between the students who performed best and the rest of the group was the teacher's expectations. As a boss, you also have the power to influence employee's performance through the expectations you set for yourself.

SETTING YOUR EXPECTATIONS

Here are seven keys that will help you set the kinds of expectations that will make you a better, if not great, boss:

1. Have clear expectations. Great bosses are not vague about the things that they want to do. Great bosses are definite about their aims and responsibilities. Be as specific as possible when setting goals.
2. Commit wholeheartedly to fulfilling your expectations. Great bosses are prepared to do what it takes to get the job done. This means that they must press on through discouragement, stand firm in trials, learn how to handle disappointment, and stay faithful when tempted.
3. Ensure that the expectation is realistic for you. Can you see yourself achieving it? Expectations must be realistic and down-to-earth too. I know that faith can move mountains and that all things are possible for those who believe. But I could never see myself beating Tiger Woods at this year's U.S. Open. No matter how much faith I have, the expectation is not viable. Occasionally we are all prone to set impractical expectations. We must be practical and see ourselves achieving the goals that we set.

4. Write down your expectations. Goals that are written down are over 20 times more likely to be achieved than goals not made explicit.
5. Write down the things that will prevent you from achieving your expectations. This keeps us vigilant and prompts us to take evasive action when our expectations are threatened. Fear, doubt, and uncertainty are just some examples of what might stop us from achieving our goals. But if we remind ourselves of these pitfalls, we will more than likely take steps to steer clear of them or deal firmly with them when they arise. Is there anything in your life that could stop you achieving the things that you have set out to do? If so, deal with the foes now.
6. Ask yourself, "What effect will achieving this expectation have on me?" If you were to reach a goal of getting a new job promotion or starting up a relationship, what effect is it going to have on you?
7. Determine how you will know when you've achieved your expectations. Do you know when your goals have been reached? They are not endless projects and responsibilities. We have to identify what success looks like. We have to acknowledge when our job is done and realize when our tasks are completed. We must know when our dreams come true and see when our vision is fulfilled.

When setting their expectations, bosses should always ask, "Is this thing right for me? Is the timing right for doing this project?" Remember, too, that different goals have different gestation periods. A chicken egg takes 21 days to break into life, a human embryo takes nine months, and an elephant takes two years. Expectations are like that. Some are accomplished quickly, some take many years.

Before these or any other objectives can be set, there needs to be planning. We need to know where we are going, why, and how we are going to get there. We need to decide what steps are necessary, when to do each one, who is going to do each one, and also how we know if we are doing it. We need to plan so that everyone is pulling in the same direction and we can accomplish specific results.

Expectations are created from the steps necessary for reaching the objective. They state what must be done, who will do it, how it will be done, when it will be done, and how well it will be done. Or, expressed another way, a planned expectation is SMART.

S = Specific—states exactly what will be accomplished

M = Measurable—how well it will be done

A = Accepted—everyone agrees on doing it this way

R = Realistic—using the resources available

T = Timed—states specifically when the goal will be met.

It is important that we always keep our purpose in mind. A man walked up to several workmen. He asked one, "What are you doing?" and the man answered, "I'm laying bricks." He addressed another, "What are you doing?" He replied, "I am installing glass." Finally he spoke to a man pushing a wheelbarrow, "What are you doing?" The man replied, "I'm building a cathedral."

Realizing that there are areas of our lives that need definite improvement, how do we go about it? Even though we realize the need to change and the value of planning and goal setting, because it's something new to us we might be reluctant to attempt it. In order for a proper and meaningful change to take place in my life, I must earnestly desire it. Another reason for initiating a change is that something severe or disastrous happening usually forces us to realize the need to change.

In order for a proper and meaningful change to take place I must set realistic and logical goals. It's similar to New Year's resolutions. Do not try to change too much at one time; work on one priority area, then add another. Remember, just as a resolution to get in shape by dieting, exercising, and losing weight will take time and effort, changing and improving my life will also take time and a real effort.

It is critical to recognize that we will stumble and fall short of our objectives, but we must not use that as an excuse to throw away our objectives or forget where we are heading and why.

6

Never Ever Make the Same Mistake Twice

Success does not consist in never making mistakes but in never making the same one a second time.
—George Bernard Shaw

It sounds so simple just to say this, "Never make the same mistake twice." All of us in our careeers are surrounded by examples of repetitive mistakes every day. This happens largely because we do not take the time to find out what really caused the original mistake and correct it. In 27 years in the railroad industry, I have seen people make their careers on this one attribute. Even when they make a mistake, there is confidence that the lesson will be learned and the issue will not reoccur.

This means that really good bosses embrace mistakes as opportunities to learn and improve. They do not sulk about what has happened; they react in an open, positive manner that keeps them in control. Their employees know it, and so do their superiors.

The difference between a singular mistake and a repetitive mistake can be the difference between a pebble and a mountain. Singular mistakes can be used to improve an organization's performance. On the other hand, repetitive mistakes can be the death knell of any organization. In short, the great boss does not make the same mistake twice.

ENCOURAGING MISTAKES

The trouble in American business is not that we are making too many mistakes, but that we are making too few. Jim Burke, former CEO of Johnson & Johnson, actually encouraged mistakes. What Burke wanted more than anything else was workers who made decisions and took risks: "If you believe that growth comes from risk taking, that you cannot grow without it, then it is essential in leading people toward growth to get them to make decisions— and to make mistakes." Mistakes are good, he said. No mistakes, no progress. Here's Burke's own story regarding a costly personal mistake:

> I once developed a new product that failed badly, and General Johnson called me in, and I was sure he was going to fire me. I had just come in late when his secretary called, and he was always in early. I can remember walking over to his office, and . . . Johnson said to me, "I understand you lost over a million dollars." And I said, "Yes, sir. That is correct." So he stood up and held out his hand. He said, "I just want to congratulate you. All business is making decisions, and if you don't make decisions, you won't have any failures. The hardest job I have is getting people to make decisions. If you make that same decision wrong again, I'll fire you. But I hope you'll make a lot of others, and that you will understand that there are going to be more failures than successes." (Wurman, 1992, p. 55)

The successful boss will profit from his mistakes and try again in a different way. The late Sam Walton, Wal-Mart's founder, knew that no company hits the target every time. That's why Wal-Mart employees aren't punished when their experiments fail. "If you learn something and you are trying something, then you probably get credit for it," Walton said once in a *Business Week* article. "But woe to the person who makes the same mistake twice." In the business world, learning from one's mistakes actually wins people over.

A boss who cannot make mistakes cannot do anything. Making mistakes is a good thing. That is how you learn. Great bosses take responsibility for them, fix them, then move on. If a boss is smart, he or she will not make that mistake again but learn from the experience.

At this point, it is no longer a mistake but education. But you still made a mistake, even though it was not a mistake—a paradox. Humility is admitting that you messed up so that you can move forward from that place. Denying your mistake is just plain denial of the truth from a place of silly pride. Doing so allows the same mistake to be made again. Pride does not serve learning, humility does. Simply stated, more bosses would learn from their mistakes if they were not so busy denying them.

In many ways, a life spent making mistakes is not only more honorable, but more useful than a life spent doing nothing. While one boss may hesitate because he feels inferior, another will be busy making mistakes and becoming superior. Unfortunately, far too many bosses often claim they do not have the time to evaluate their mistakes. We would argue that you do not *not* have the time.

In most cases, those exceptional bosses who do not repeat their mistakes are good problem solvers. They take the time to really determine the true root cause of the mistake, and they fix it, or they ask for help. With them, it does not happen again. Great bosses recognize the truth and admit it to themselves. They understand that making a mistake is nothing, it is just an experience.

Mistakes happen. We exist in an imperfect world, where choices have many consequences So mistakes exist, absolutely. When mistakes happen, bosses must repair them, if possible. All great bosses have made lots of mistakes, but the mark of a great boss is to admit mistakes and not make the same mistake twice. "Fool me once, shame on you; fool me twice, shame on me."

THE VALUE OF MISTAKES

Without mistakes, innovation in business is virtually impossible. Ideas become great programs and products because of trial and error. It would be a mistake to try to avoid all mistakes. Indeed, it would be a colossal blunder to attempt doing things right the first time, every time. In today's light-speed economy ("new" economy and "old" economy), if you do not fall on your face both regularly and painfully, you are likely to end up dead instead. The only people not making mistakes are ones playing their game without risk and without novelty and without progress. If your company cannot accommodate, even reward, failure, in the long run it cannot succeed.

Doing things wrong is the number one—perhaps the only—source of innovation. Enlightened trial and error beats the planning of flawless intellects. The reason is simple: The best solutions to most problems are rarely the most obvious. Mistakes are the portals of discovery. Think about it. What did you ever learn by doing something right the first time? Because the road to success is paved with failures, the faster you move through them, the faster you might find a way that works. Do not prolong the agony, get it over with quickly, learn the most you can, and move on. We fail faster to succeed sooner.

World leaders and scientists have a wonderful legacy of being wrong in a big way. Edison's tolerance for mistakes is renowned. The European discovery of America was a mistake. Even the invention of Teflon came by way of a mistake. Great companies also have a long and gallant history of failing. AMC's Gremlin was a big flop, but it paved the way for the ever-popular hatchback. There are many famous failed computers, including Apple's Lisa and Newton or the Palm Pilot's predecessor, Zoomer—evidence that failures breed innovations rather than stifle them. Not all business failures are so glorious. Sixty-five out of 100 business startups vanish without a trace within 5 years, and 90 percent are gone within 10 years. But we need these failures—without them there would be no companies to survive.

If you are in the surgery business or fly airplanes for a living, you may not want to make any mistakes. But for the rest of us, doing things wrong is prerequisite to doing things right. As the philosopher Ludwig Wittgenstein (1984) said, "If people did not sometimes do silly things, nothing intelligent would ever get done." Many companies say they encourage mistakes, but they really intimidate and punish the mistake-makers. As soon as you begin to do that, you foster a better-safe-than-sorry attitude. Instead, put your money where your mouth is. What about having a regular meeting dissecting the mistakes of the month, trying to learn their lessons. Train people to savor their mistakes, and understand the strange paths that led them astray.

When things go wrong, do you sound a hunt for the guilty? Do not cast blame—commemorate mistake makers as heroes. One of the reasons mistakes go undetected—and progress slowed—is that people are not willing to take credit for their errors. Rather than call attention to things that are off course (and risk their careers), they prefer to bury them for as long as possible.

When your car breaks down, do you blame the driver, or do you just fix the problem? When a project or a process is veering off course, treat it like a breakdown. Rather than spending time deciding who did what wrong, do this: Restate where you want to go and figure out what will get you back on track.

Create a company of learners with a formal debriefing policy. Without one, learning from mistakes is just one more accident. Debrief everything—good, bad, or indifferent. Use the four-stage catechism of the learning organization: What worked? What did not work? What was missing? What do we do next?

One way to really get things moving on a project is to declare a state of emergency. Emergencies mobilize people. They bring out the whatever-it-takes attitude, especially when they know that mistakes will be tolerated and that mistake makers will be lionized. That's exactly why I ask my staff to report each month at least one mistake.

You may find it strange to know that comedian John Cleese of Monty Python fame has written and produced several business training films. "In organizations where mistakes are not admitted, you get two types of counterproductive behavior," Cleese has said. "First, since mistakes are 'bad,' if they are committed by people at the top, the feedback arising from those mistakes has to be ignored or selectively reinterpreted—in order that those top people can pretend that no mistake has been made. So it does not get fixed. Second, if they are committed by people lower down in the organization, mistakes get concealed." In other words, if we create a culture where mistakes are intolerable, those mistakes will never get fixed because they'll never be identified. We'll end up creating a culture absent of innovation and overflowing with cover-up.

As leaders, bosses' credibility is on the line whenever they fail to admit a mistake. In fact, the biggest mistake a boss can make is not taking responsibility for a mistake. This is done in a variety of ways: by pointing the finger at somebody else; by making excuses; by spinning the blunder into something that's not a big deal. If a boss habitually covers up mistakes rather than owns up to them, that boss loses credibility. And that's when a boss loses impact.

LEARNING FROM MISTAKES

According to Paul Orfalea, founder and CEO of Kinko's, not learning from our mistakes is often due to lack of reflection.

> When I make a mistake, I usually mull over it at night and think about the would've, could've, should've stuff. But then I move on. It's important to reflect and analyze, but then we all have to realize that what's done is done, so move on—tomorrow is a new day. (Godin, 2002, p. 5)

It is imperative that we bosses learn from our mistakes. When we do not, we are bound to frustrate others, which may lead to loss of future responsibilities and opportunities. Repeating mistakes also could have long-term negative impacts, not only on our personal reputations, but also on the reputation of our organizations.

How Old Are Your Wineskins?

In the familiar Mark 2:22 passage, Jesus says, "No one pours new wine into old wineskins. If he does, the wine will burst the skins, and both the wine and the wineskins will be ruined. No, he pours new wine into new wineskins." The attitude "We've always done it that way" is the mentality of old wineskins—and the mentality of those who are afraid of making mistakes, afraid of failing.

Fighting the People Pleasers

Great bosses are not people pleasers. They understand that taking risks can alienate people. But they also see that failing to take risks can wipe out an organization faster than almost any other single factor. Great bosses

- like to rock the boat.
- do not tend to play it safe.
- are more concerned with progress than peace.
- rarely, if ever, crumble under opposition.
- rarely, if ever, have difficulty making decisions.
- are not overly concerned about being liked.
- do not look to others for approval of their ideas.
- never lack courage.

When we look at a great boss, we see someone who is anything but a people pleaser, someone who is concerned only about doing the right things. Sometimes the smartest mistakes are those that you make yourself—simply because it's the right thing to do.

A great boss is willing to offend others if it means taking risks. We believe that the fear of making mistakes and the fear of failure can cripple an organization, or at least hold it back from greater potential. We all probably like to think that our organization is on the cutting edge of our industry. Yet, ask yourself whether that pioneer spirit has been lost and has been co-opted by safety and comfort first?

MAKING SMARTER MISTAKES

Let's be honest: More of us are making bigger decisions in less time—and with less information—than ever. That is why, almost of necessity, we are messing up more than ever. The flip side of making progress is making mistakes. "If you're not making mistakes, you're not taking risks, and that means you're not going anywhere," argues John W. Holt, Jr., co-author of *Celebrate Your Mistakes* (1996). "The key is to make errors faster than the competition, so you have more chances to learn and win" (p. 94). An utterly reasonable proposition—and one that most of us routinely ignore.

Perhaps the most widely embraced delusion in business today is that it is possible (or even desirable) to create organizations where mistakes are rare, rather than a necessary cost of doing business. The problem with embracing this delusion: It encourages you to hide mistakes, shift the blame for them, or pretend they are something else.

Mistakes can be great learning opportunities, They show cracks—areas of vulnerability—where you do not pay the price now but might later. How can you make smarter mistakes? Admit them quickly. The cover-up is always worse than the crime. It is the favorite aphorism of Washington politicians— nearly all of whom ignore their own advice the moment something goes wrong. But businesspeople do not have to play by inside-the-Beltway rules. The surest way to defuse a mistake is to fess up to it—early. Do not wait to tell the people who need to know.

In some companies, even those serious about learning from mistakes, the M-word itself is taboo. It simply carries too much baggage. People tend to prefer euphemisms such as "teachable moment." Most of us are brought up to think of mistakes as a bad thing. Taking personal responsibility is a basic test of in-the-trenches leadership. The leaders above you do not want to hear excuses, and they certainly do not respect buck-passing. Indeed, precisely because it is so rare, taking ownership of a mistake is a powerful way to exude a sense of accountability. You demonstrate that you have things under control and that you are a leader. People will forget the mistake, but they will remember your behavior.

TURNING MISTAKES INTO KNOWLEDGE

Every great boss is a learner. The moment you stop learning, you stop leading. And learning comes from knowledge. According to *Webster's Dictionary*, knowledge is "the fact or condition of knowing something with familiarity gained through experience or association." Knowledge is the richness of learning, insight, and experience that is in people's heads (and some say in their bodies). Knowledge allows you to take action and make decisions. Knowledge can be in people's heads (tacit knowledge), or it can be written down or recorded (explicit knowledge). You can never capture the full richness or complexity of what's in people's heads. Try writing down the knowledge of how to ride a bicycle, for example, and then give the document to your child to learn from instead of holding the bicycle seat when they take their first ride!

Explicit knowledge can be a good catalyst for connecting people together, as it can be stored and searched. Some captured knowledge can be of enormous value if easy to share, easy to read, and easy to add to, and if it provides a connection to others who know. For an organization, knowledge is the combination of critical information and collective intellect that enables an organization to make a decision, create a solution, or change a direction. And knowledge comes most often from learning from our mistakes.

Mistakes are a fact of life. Forget about total quality and zero defects. You cannot afford it, especially in this day and age. There is a level of quality beyond which mistakes are a viable economic alternative. Unless the outcome of your product or service impacts life or death, the cost of perfection cannot be justified. It is the response to imperfection that counts and provides us with knowledge.

There will be times we are rigid when we should be loose, loose when we should be firm; times we are inconsistent or unfair. All of us will make judgments based on the best knowledge we have at the time, only to find out later that we were wrong. Yet whenever we do something we have not done before, we inevitably make mistakes. It is part of the learning curve.

"WRONG" IS OFTEN "RIGHT"

Wrong answers are at the heart of the scientific discovery process. By discovering what's wrong, through exploring and examining what does not work, we eventually figure out what does work. Mistakes are critical building blocks in the problem-solving process. When learning to walk, falling down is as important as getting up. Many of us have not had an opportunity to learn to appreciate mistakes as opportunities for growth. When we make a mistake, we judge ourselves harshly. Mistakes do not fit in with our vision of ourselves as perfect parents. But perfection—even if achievable—is not what is needed from a boss. It is better for an organization to have bosses who demonstrate how to keep growing despite human frailties.

Employees watch their bosses carefully. Through their example, bosses can teach that how they deal with their mistakes is more important than the fact that a mistake was made. Great bosses acknowledge their mistakes in a reasonable way. If we make an error and respond by saying, "Oh no! I made a mistake! I'll never try that again!" we teach our employees that mistakes are insurmountable. If, on the other hand, we say, "Well, that didn't work. I guess I'll have to figure out a different way," we give our employees an incredible statement of optimism.

Remember that being able to correct yourself is a real sign of strength. Admitting mistakes takes courage. Although it is important to acknowledge mistakes, it is not enough to say, "Oops! I blew it. Sorry!" If we stop there, there is nothing to keep us from repeating the same mistake again. If we really want to change, we need to make the critical leap from acknowledging our mistakes to doing something about them.

Tell your employees or your boss what you are going to do: Include them in the problem-solving process. Most people love to come up with ideas, and their suggestions can be quite useful.

7

Go to Your Boss with Your Action Plan, Not Your Problem

All mankind is divided into three classes: those that are immovable, those that are movable, and those that move.
—Benjamin Franklin

In most cases, your superior already knows there is a particular problem in your domain. If you go to your boss with a symptom of the problem, you will probably have a solution imposed upon you. Who knows better than you what the solution is and how to implement it? Great bosses understand that they must get to the essence of a challenge and develop an action plan in order to solve it. Such a principle is rooted in pragmatism, not politics.

BUILDING THE BRIDGE

In 1966, the only way to cross the 4 1/2-mile-wide Columbia River that forms the border between Oregon and Washington was to take a ferry. It was a beautiful ride through the splendor of the Pacific Northwest as the ferryboat plied the river's waters. But it was also a time-consuming, two-hour ride. Then someone had a vision—build a bridge that would span the river.

The debate was fierce. "Too costly," some said.

"How will we pay for it?" others asked.

Still others stated, "This bridge doesn't connect any two cities, so why build it?"

But the vision persisted, and the project began. As the bridge progressed, scoffers gave it a name: the bridge to nowhere. Today, that "bridge to nowhere"—the Astoria-Megler Bridge—carries more than 2 million cars annually between Oregon and Washington.

In contrast, during the same years, there truly was a "bridge to nowhere" in Pittsburgh, Pennsylvania. An off-ramp of the parkway system in that city extended out into one of the rivers and ended abruptly with barricades. For years it sat there connecting the riverbank with nothing. Across the country there have been other bridges that were never completed and became nothing more than conversation pieces or the focus of political haggling.

Bridges work only if they connect two different places. The same is true with vision. Without a plan of action, our vision for what we might become as a boss becomes just another bridge to nowhere.

CONVERTING A VISION INTO AN ACTION PLAN

Two common questions often emerge once a vision has been articulated: "How do I convert the ideas on paper or in my mind into decisions and actions that will make a difference?" and "How do I use the vision to lead and bring about needed change?" A partial but important answer to these questions is this: It takes an action plan.

Any enterprise is built by wise planning, becomes strong through common sense, and profits wonderfully by keeping abreast of the facts. Visions need plans to bring them to life. A written, communicated, and widely owned vision statement is a "bridge to nowhere" without an action plan. An action plan converts ideas into decisions that reallocate the resources of your organization to undergird the new vision.

One of the first challenges of a great boss is making sure that the right people are in the right places, doing the right things. Finding the right fit with people and responsibilities goes deeper than the traditional steps in hiring, promoting, or orienting someone to a new position. You must know how the job fits into the total organization, the role of the position, and the performance skills or competencies demanded on the job. Perhaps even more important than the performance skills (most of these can be taught, after all) are the personal attitudes, knowledge, qualities, aptitudes, and natural strengths that best fit at three levels: the individual/job function level, the work group, and the broader organizational culture level. This idea of person/job fit is not simply a matter of how much any one person is like the job, or like other people who do the same job. Rather, it also has to do with synergy between people and the need for certain tensions and diversity to exist in order to maintain a certain aliveness and vitality into the future.

A key pitfall to avoid is writing an action plan and then doing things the same as always. Without a plan of action, a solution is simply the fruit of putting dreams on paper. It might as well be made into a paper airplane and flown into a shredder.

To build trust, to maintain credibility, and to honor those who participated, your vision statement must move from written words into new decisions, new strategy and tactics (when needed), reallocated human and financial resources, and change. A vision that lacks concrete decisions leading to actions will never result in people hearing the message that can alter your organization.

I have found that there are four key questions that good leaders need to answer for the people they are to lead:

1. Where are we?
2. Where are going?
3. How are we going to get there?
4. What is in it for me?

These tips can help craft your leadership message and communicate your vision to your employees:

1. *Where are we?* Sell the message that you have a good company, good people, and a good plan. The vision is to make the company better.

2. *Where are we going?* Talk about competition if you must, but stress improving your customer outcomes. In many cases, your number-one competitor is yourself.

3. *How are we going to get there?* Be specific about objectives, action steps, and timetables.

4. *What is in it for me?* Spell out how your staff will benefit—from paychecks to job security. Be detailed and specific.

Each one of these needs to be addressed on a daily basis. Moreover, we need to make sure that everybody in the organization knows the answer to each of the questions. Successful leaders constantly ask, "What are our goals and mission? What constitutes performance and brings results in the organization?" Making sure that the employees understand the company's mission more greatly ensures their loyalty and ability to serve customers.

GOALS VERSUS OBJECTIVES

In my experience, I have witnessed far too many bosses who have failed to grasp the differences between a goal and an objective. Bosses abound who have put forth a laudable goal—say, to increase market share of a new product line. And the boss has a plan—pick a hole in the market that is not being filled and attack it. But this is where things usually go awry and get fuzzy. Most bosses have only a general idea of how to accomplish their goal. Too often there is no real set of objectives in place to see how the goal is attained.

Objectives are tangible accomplishments that can be easily measured and that move toward the goal step-by-step. Focus on a series of objectives that are concrete and realizable to get to the goal.

An action plan is a contract that you make with your boss that identifies those steps you agree to take in an effort to alleviate or solve a challenge.

Process is everything. You can have the right vision, the right idea. You can even have the right result. But if your action plan is wrong, you will have a disaster.

The plan must be tailored to your individual needs and circumstances. As you consider developing your plan, focus on eliminating self-defeating patterns of behavior. Action plans are designed to move you from reactive thinking to proactive thinking, from pessimism to optimism, from passive behavior to active behavior, and from a mode of following to a mode of leading. The goals and actions in your plan must be expressed in daily and weekly activities. This will result in activities that appear less daunting and fearful. It is also a good strategy to overcome procrastination.

Also, be patient. Behavioral change, physical change, environmental change, social change, and interpersonal change are all most healthfully achieved gradually. To anticipate or plan for abrupt change or instant success is another self-defeating behavior facilitated by our contemporary culture emphasizing instant gratification.

There are certain characteristics that are necessary in your action plan.

- The plan must be in writing.
- Most important, the plan must be challenging but realistic and doable. Designing a plan that is impossible to implement is just another self-defeating behavior. However, designing a plan that does not challenge you to address the issues you identified in your self-inventory is a sign of more passive behavior.
- Items in your plan must require you to take action!
- Action items must be measurable.
- The plan must require you to evaluate your progress daily. Three major obstacles to achieving goals must be avoided in your daily evaluation: procrastination ("I'll get to that tomorrow"); rationalization ("It really wasn't that important"); and blaming others ("My boss gave me a new assignment so I didn't have time today"—classic examples of excuses that hinder action-plan achievement.

Your role is to accept responsibility, offer viable solutions, and adjust your behavior for more effective goal achievement. If you do this on a daily basis, you will make gradual and incremental progress toward your ultimate goal of being a great boss.

Assuming that you have worked hard to communicate your vision to your people as well as to your boss, here are the steps to create an action plan:

1. Put together an action team. Ideally, the team that helped develop the vision is a good place to start. But consider

adding to it key colleagues, department heads, or staff who will help live out the vision action plan.

2. Walk through the vision statement and identify the key ideas or initiatives. A simple way to do this is to identify key action phrases such as, "We envision that our idea of customer service will entail truly serving customers."

3. Prioritize the vision ideas. Identify those ideas that you sense you need to tackle first, second, third, and so on, because of their strategic importance to your organization's vitality.

4. Assign a leader or a team to each of these priorities. Nothing of substance will happen unless you do this. Every priority needs a leader. If you do not have enough leaders to cover all the priorities, launch only those for which you have leadership. This step requires discernment, so you may need to expand the leadership potential in your organization. It is difficult to decide how many priorities to have. Three to seven are probably about all that any one group can handle. Focus on a few things that are doable rather than try to implement your entire vision at once. Set a date six months in the future to convene the team to decide whether you can add any new priorities at that time.

5. Empower (give the authority and the responsibility to) your leaders or teams to develop each of the priorities. Challenge them to think outside the box. This strategic thinking is critical to breakthroughs.

MORE ON EMPOWERMENT

The past twenty years have shown a steady increase in participation in decision-making at work. Authority and decision-making have moved closer to the people on the front lines. Though not yet dominant, we have seen substantial growth in high-performance workplaces, self-managed work groups, and democratic work practices. Central to the effectiveness of increased participation is the ability to see people rather than simply employees, human capital, or human resources. When we recognize our workplaces as communities of people working toward common goals and benefits, we also shift our thinking from how best to motivate people to how we can better engage people. Great bosses cease doing things to people at work and begin working with a more collaborative spirit. As we often say at BNSF, "Empowerment isn't something we grant or withhold from people here. . . . People are naturally empowered. They come to us empowered. My job is to help them uncover all that that means."

Without empowerment, all human endeavors are prone to take the path of least resistance, which rarely leads to new vitality. Once empowerment is activated, goals can be set, action steps laid out, people assigned, and calendars and budgets established.

It never ceases to amaze me how many leaders fail to empower the people they are leading. Some think that employees cannot be trusted with particular information about the company or to perform a particular task. Others think that employees are not smart enough or able to grasp new ideas or concepts. Still others manipulate employees so that they can control them.

Teddy Roosevelt (1910) probably said it best when he stated, "The best executive is the one that has sense enough to pick good men to do what he wants done and self-restraint enough to keep from meddling with them while they're doing it." That is what empowerment is all about.

Empowering employees is crucial because there is no way any company can write a manual that gives the answer on how to deal with every situation. Employees have to be empowered and trusted to use their best judgment when serving the interests of the organization.

I have a friend who gives what he calls the "Three-Legged Stool Test" to his employees when they make an empowered decision. He trains them to ask three questions:

1. Is this decision good for our customer?
2. Is this decision good for our employees?
3. Is this decision good for our company?

The answers to these questions serve as the litmus test for employees on whether to take action or not.

It is hard work to turn your vision into action, but it is not impossible. It will go better if the action plans you lay out are pursued with gusto. Your vision simply will not come to life without the blessing of your boss. Visions come to life as committed people build a bridge together—to enhance the organization's performance. Some of that work will include insight and thought. Some of it will mean taking risks. It will require you to sort the treasures from the baggage and even the garbage that has built up in your organization. Some of the work will require that you stay the course. Whatever the work, bridge building will connect what you want your organization to become and what it will be.

But always remember, being a great boss does not mean being popular. As Peter Drucker (quoted in Melendez, 1996) says, "An effective leader is not someone who is loved or admired. He or she is someone whose followers do the right things. Popularity is not leadership. Results are." Remember that the ultimate goal is to get people to do what you want done because they *want* to do it (p. 76).

As a leader, getting your message through to a cynical audience is near to impossible. Instead, recognize the critical importance of being "on message," telling the same story over and over again. A word of wisdom: when you get sick of telling it, you are probably just beginning to get your message out.

Great bosses recognize the fact that they are highly visible. Therefore, they set good examples. Drucker again:

> They submitted themselves to the "mirror test"—that is, they made sure that the person they saw in the mirror in the morning was the kind of person they wanted to be, respect, and believe in. This way the way they fortified themselves against the leader's greatest temptations—to do things that are popular rather than right and to do petty, mean, sleazy things. (Melendez, 1996, p. 124)

I learned early in my career that in order to maintain control of my operation, I had to appear as though I was in control. If the operation was running rough, I led off with my plan of attack before I even stated that we were in trouble. This worked. I had few occasions where my superiors would take over and dictate a plan. They did not have to; I was in control.

At that same time, I saw many of my colleagues who were in the same situation with their particular operations articulate to the letter exactly what had happened, who, what, and when. They failed to mention the why or what they were going to do about it. They spent way more time telling about what had happened and what was going on, but never stated what they were going to do about it. They usually got a plan forced down their throat. Their people knew that the plan did not come from their boss but from higher up in the company. This did not promote credibility in their boss. They were labeled as news reporters, not news-makers.

Let's face it. Most great bosses are walking problem solvers. If they hear a problem, they try to solve it. If they hear a solution and action plan, they might offer a suggestion, but most of the time they trust that the situation is under control. I have found this to be universal, even with the toughest bosses.

It comes back to maintaining control, and your people seeing that you are in control. It is easy to tell the difference between a corrective action-plan developed and implemented by your boss and one driven from higher up. We have all been involved in action plans driven from top management. Whether they work or not is not the issue. The issue is that people want a boss who is in control; they want a decision-maker. They do not want a puppet or a messenger. Great bosses solve their problems with their solutions, and their employees know it.

8

Follow-Up

It is easy to dodge our responsibilities, but we cannot dodge
the consequences of dodging our responsibilities.
                                            —Josiah Stamp

Corporate America, for the most part, is lousy at follow-up. I run
across people who are able to demonstrate visionary thinking,
can deliver motivating speeches, and have good people skills. But
my observation is that most of corporate America is just plain
terrible when it comes to following up on assigned action items,
returning calls, keeping commitments, time management, and the
like. Anyone come to mind? Perhaps your boss? Perhaps someone
on your team? Perhaps you?

I came to the point one day when I realized that I was lousy at
follow-up. Too many important things were slipping through the
cracks, such as things that mattered to me—that I really wanted
to do someday but just never could find the time. I had signed up
to do these things but just couldn't seem to figure out how to fit
them in with everything else on my plate—things that needed my
attention.

I had all sorts of excuses. Maybe you've heard yourself utter
something similar: "I'm just not wired up to be organized!" "I
don't have time to get this figured out—I just need to do it!" "I'm
not that bad. I know where everything is." "If that thing is so
important, it will raise its ugly head somewhere down the road!"

I eventually realized that life had scaled much faster than my ability to keep up with it—increasing job responsibilities, more staff, more complex projects, new house, kids, baseball, soccer, serving in the community and church. The so-called American Dream is leading many people to exclaim the American Scream: "I can't keep up!"

"I'll get back to you on that." "The check is in the mail." "Let's do lunch." All are examples of clichés that we really don't count on happening. Unfortunately, this happens too regularly in business. In fact it happens so regularly that when they do get back to us, we do get the check the next day, or we actually get together for lunch, we are surprised. Follow-up is one of the most cherished attributes of a great boss.

In all of my conversations with great bosses, this one really seems to get them going with reference to the best bosses they have ever had. "Bob was the best boss I ever had; his follow-up was incredible." People like bosses with follow-up. They know things are going to get done, and they know they are going to be part of it.

John Kotter of Harvard Business School regularly tells a story about GE's Jack Welch in terms of follow-up. Professor Kotter had a group of business leaders together for a daylong session on leadership. Jack Welch was in the group. As Kotter began his presentation using overheads, he saw a hand raised among the group. It was Jack's hand, and he asked the question, "Are we going to get copies of these overheads?" Kotter responded that sure they could get copies of the overheads. Just as he began to go on with his presentation, he noticed that Jack's hand was again raised with a question, "When will we get copies of the overheads?" The professor responded that after the session, he would have one of his assistants make copies of the overheads, and to appear that he was beginning to get the picture with regard to Jack's obvious concern for the documents, he added, "and I'll have them overnighted to your office."

Thinking he had this issue put to rest, he again began his presentation only to once again see the familiar hand in the air. "If you have your assistant make the copies now, she can give them to us and then we will be sure that we will get them and it will save you the expense of overnight delivery." Jack had followed up on the issue and now he was ready to go on to enjoy the presentation.

We have all heard the phrase, "I'll get back to you on that." We hear it so often with no follow-up that when someone actually does get back to us, it is a shock. We have also heard open-ended action items that do not include a time limit. Statements such as, "We'll have to get together and work on that" are not nearly as direct as "Let's get together in my office at four o'clock this afternoon and announce our decision at the staff meeting tomorrow." Just adding the phrase "by close of business today" implies that follow-up is present and the job will get done. Great bosses walk and talk the daily mantra of follow-up. Their employees know it, their bosses know it.

Great bosses know that by avoiding the responsibility for their own behavior, they give that responsibility to some other individual or organization or entity. But this means that they then give away their power to that entity.

A common mistake that bosses make is committing to do something and not following up on it. This absolutely destroys credibility. It does not take long before they are not taken seriously. A boss cannot stand to lose integrity over follow-up.

We can tell early on in the careers of our frontline managers whether or not they possess the attribute of follow-up. Normally they fall into the trap of trying to please everyone and telling them what they want to hear. They would like to say "yes" to everything. They do not realize that saying "yes" and then failing to deliver means a blow to their integrity. Even saying "It will never happen again" is a commitment heard at all levels of an organization for which there is a considerable amount of poor follow-up.

"It will never happen again" can get about as common and as trite as "The check is in the mail," especially in groups who do not value follow-up. In the end, if you can do it, state that you are going to do it with a date and time. If you cannot do it, say what you can do about it with a date and time. For either of these paths, when the date and time come, have it done.

Follow-up breeds follow-up. Either you do it or you do not. It is addictive. It is contagious. It starts at the top. It starts with the boss. Whether it is close of business today, tomorrow, Friday, end of the month, end of the quarter, end of the year, setting an exact moment that follow-up will be completed is a good sign that follow-up is being practiced.

Early in my career I remember hearing a story about a high-level meeting between executives of the company I was working for at the time and one of our largest customers. We had developed a new transportation product that was going to improve service dramatically, lower costs and prices, as well as provide a safer operation. It seemed too good to be true. We needed the customer to buy in to the proposal to make it work. After the presentation was over, the decision maker within the customer group cleared his throat and made a statement to the effect that we had shown them an interesting proposal and that they would have a team take a look at it, study the benefits, and then get back to us with their answer. Our leader, a person whom all of us respected very much, stood up and said, "Study it all you want, starts tonight!" And it did.

In our company we place great value on follow-up. Failing to follow up on a commitment is something we take very seriously. All our managers know this. We like to believe that when we say something is going to happen, it does, and our employees know it. Our union leaders also know that we place great value on follow-up, and second only to doing the right thing for the right reasons, follow-up and follow-through on commitments is one of the things they hold us accountable for.

Follow-up is a regular topic of conversation among managers at United Parcel Service. In a business where time is everything and there are several deadlines every day, making commitments is a must. They also stick out like a sore thumb when they do not happen.

Employees respect a boss who follows up. They know that when a problem occurs, if the boss says it will be fixed, it will. That's what defines great boss. At its core, follow-up is honoring your commitments. If you say you're going to do something, then simply do it.

Great bosses viscerally know this and communicate that reality. They know that no successful action plan is complete without true follow-up. Great bosses establish parameters that clearly define roles and responsibilities for their people. Everybody is certain as to who does what, when, and how. Great bosses understand that many action plans require adjustments and catalysts. As a result, they create a dynamic culture of adaptation and flexibility.

THE VALUE OF FOLLOW-UP

Follow-up can be defined as the process of giving continued attention to something you said you were going to do. Simply put, follow-up is a process of continual attention, which literally means work on a consistent basis. All too often, however, bosses have many people ask them to follow-up on something and nothing is ever really done.

The goal of follow-up is to see something carried through to the end. It involves seeing the whole picture. The wheel illustration provides a guide. At the center of the wheel—the hub—is our reputation, around which our credibility as a boss revolves. The rim is where the wheel touches the road and is also visible to all. The spokes on a turning wheel are invisible, but vitally necessary to get power from the hub to the rim. They must be balanced for the wheel to roll smoothly. The spokes are those things that must be followed up on to keep the wheel turning properly. Neglect one spoke, and the entire wheel is thrown out of balance.

Effective follow-up involves having clear goals, having a plan for accomplishing those goals, and then putting it all in to action. A great boss realizes that follow-up can bring these tangible benefits:

• To establish confidence in your ability as a boss
• To help create credibility and a buy-in of your action plan
• To help the entire organization to better understand what kinds of things you want to do
• To take responsibility for growth

A great boss has the privilege of providing care and direction for the people around him or her. Follow-up involves the impartation of principles, as well as the example of what a great boss is and does. Remember that consistency causes growth within an organization. Understanding this principle is critical to follow-up characterized by trusting what you do as a boss rather than by becoming anxious and indecisive.

As you become involved in follow-up, it will soon become apparent to you that, although you may teach everyone the same material, each individual is unique and has different questions. Therefore your follow-up with one individual will never be exactly like that of any other. Sometimes it may take meeting three or four times to effectively communicate assurance of the issue, whereas at other times a person may grasp the action very quickly. Be sensitive to the person and his particular needs. Do not feel that you have to fit everything into a rigid structure or schedule.

9

The Great Boss
as Team Builder

Let no man imagine that he has no influence. Whoever he
may be, and wherever he may be placed, the man who thinks
becomes a light and a power.
—Henry George

Organizations are the amalgamation of teams—both large and
small—that interact with each other from both the inside and
the outside. In many ways, the ability of these teams to work
together toward a common vision can be the ultimate determinant of success or failure for an organization. Clearly the ways
teams are lead will have a major impact upon the accomplishments or otherwise of the team.

When asked what they want from a team leader, most people
will often identify several values they want the team builder to
hold.

- Commitment to people as well as the task
- Desire to support and serve the team as well as to lead from
  the front
- Enthusiasm, energy, inspiration, and sufficient expertise
- Willingness to shoulder responsibility rather than pass the
  buck
- Ability to make the team come together to achieve more than
  a group of individuals

Great bosses are such individuals. They embody at least some if not all of these characteristics.

Commitment to People

Most team members are primarily concerned about relationships and about being valued as a team member, before they are concerned about the task that the team is to undertake. Feeling secure in a group environment is an important prerequisite before individual contribution. The good team leader is able to spend time building the team, not only when the team starts off, but also when a newcomer joins an existing team.

Desire to Support and Serve

While team members want to see the ability to lead from the front, they are also strongly motivated by the ability to lead from the back! There is a balance to be struck between a willingness to take on any chores that need to be done by the team and taking an inappropriate balance of roles so that the leadership is diminished.

Enthusiasm, Energy, Inspiration, and Expertise

Unsurprisingly, team members want to be inspired and motivated by a team leader who has the energy and enthusiasm to fire them up. However, they also want to feel secure that the team leader has, or has access to, the necessary expertise to lead the team in the right direction. The leader does not have to be the most knowledgeable about the subject at hand, but if the leader is not, he or she must encourage the input of others.

Willingness to Shoulder Responsibility

Team leaders are tested under pressure. When challenges arise, as they inevitably will, the leader needs to take responsibility to ensure that they are met as far as possible and that the team is strengthened as a result. This does not mean that the leaders should admit that issues beyond their control are in any way their fault (although they should be honest in admitting their mistakes), but rather they should adopt a proactive stance to ensure that the team is not deflected from its course.

Ability to Achieve More as a Team

Teams only become a team once there is some synergy within the group. The team process adds value to that which a disparate group of individuals would achieve undirected.

THE RIGHT ATTITUDES ABOUT TEAM BUILDING

I have discovered that great bosses become great team builders when they develop the right attitudes.

Attitude 1: Unconditional Acceptance

The first attitude, or approach, that serves as the foundation for a strong team is unconditionality. Show me two people or more trying to work together and I'll show you a group of individuals who are flawed. Each possesses his or her own individual strengths, weaknesses, prejudices, quirks, suspicions, bad habits, hot buttons, frustrations, and baggage. The key is to accept that other person, warts and all.

After all, when two or more parties want to develop a relationship together, the single greatest challenge is often accepting each other for who they are, not what the others want them to be. Too often, however, I find that people think that somehow, some way we can change the other person to fit exactly what we want and need. Bluntly put, this thinking is flawed and simply does not work. It is like trying to teach a pig to sing. In the end, all you do is get muddy and annoy the pig.

It is not necessary to like everything about the other person in order for the team to be successful. In fact, it is impossible. Everyone has his or her shortcomings, even you. Now I'm not trying to intentionally lower your self-esteem. However, I can assure you that other parties on the team do not like everything

about you either. Lasting teams acknowledge the inevitable im-
perfections in each participant and yet still move forward. In fact,
honest differences are often a healthy sign of progress.

Attitude 2: Unwavering Commitment

A great boss goes into the team-building process with an iron
will and a constant, faithful determination to see the team succeed. Great bosses eliminate the word "try" when it comes to their
teams. People who "try" are actually leaving an escape hatch
open for the likely possibility that the relationship will fail. On
your next commercial flight, would you like to hear the captain
announce that he is going to "try" to land the plane when he gets
the chance? Great bosses commit to make their teams work from
the onset. No trying.

Attitude 3: Unswerving Dedication

Although a great boss can control her personal involvement
in the team, she knows she can influence 100 percent of it. This
is comparable to serving ham and eggs for breakfast. The
chicken was involved, but the pig was committed. The great
bosses give a 24/7 commitment to their teams every day in
every way. Giving anything less than 100% is a sure prescription
for failure.

Attitude 4: Undeviating Contribution

No team will ever be "fair" in the sense that it will be balanced
and evened out every time. At the risk of sounding presumptu-
ous, I am a confessed giver. Most of my relationships are heavily
slanted toward my business associates. I firmly believe that one
of the reasons I was successful in building the kinds of effective
teams I had over the past decades is because of this desire to go
beyond merely being fair.

Similarly, do not treat people "nicely." Grow your teams by
putting your partners on a mental pedestal and spoiling them like
crazy. Seek to meet their needs that must be and should be
satisfied.

Attitude 5: Unlimited Productivity

The more you can recognize people's needs, the more you can understand the connection between what you bring and what they need, and the more likely you are to build a successful team based on solutions. A real dialogue with someone in a team environment is not a bargain-basement transaction with haggling and bickering, a low form of negotiation. Neither is it a situation in which A confronts B in a contest, but a conversation in which each presents facts and each considers the other's facts. It is a reasonable exchange of ideas, bringing into being a new body of knowledge.

I call this the making of the third mind. That is, when a solution is reached, it is the product of one mind combined with a second mind that creates a new and more dynamic third mind. The solution is no longer theirs or mine, but instead, it is *ours*.

Attitude 6: Unconstrained Communication

The greatest problem of communication is to assume that it took place. Do not assume that the other parties on your team know how much you care and that they matter. Assumptions are the termites of relationships. It is incumbent for you to constantly demonstrate and prove to them what they are getting out of the relationship. People tend to forget quickly and can become lulled to sleep by a sense of comfort and ease. Always remind those on your teams what benefits they are deriving day in and day out from knowing you. The best way to do this is by showing them.

Attitude 7: Unreserved Optimism

Dale Carnegie (1990) said, "It is easy to criticize, condemn, and complain, and most people do." Great bosses assure strong and healthy relationships by becoming the most upbeat, optimistic persons around. Because your team members already agonize over their faults and weaknesses, they do not need you to remind them again. In many cases, the best advice might be "Never miss a good chance to shut up." Shower your associates with positive feedback and sensible compliments and then watch what happens to your relationships.

Attitude 8: Undaunted Respect

Be very cautious about exploiting your teammates with others. When in doubt, I have found it is best to err on the side of caution. I have not yet met the person who wants her teamwork to be used, exploited, and abused. Respecting both your associates and the team you mutually share will go a long way to preserving its strength and longevity.

SOME COMMON MISTAKES TOWARD TEAM BUILDING

From my experience, I have witnessed several well-intentioned bosses who approach their teams in the wrong ways. Following are a few common mistakes I have seen.

Assuming an Average Commitment Level

For the average team member, commitment means "I come to meetings and respond to anything I'm supposed to vote on. If something doesn't happen, it isn't my fault."

In addition, the traditional time commitment is usually inadequate. Most teams assume a handful of people meeting once a month can bring a new direction or change. In most instances that would not provide even minimal maintenance.

Meeting Too Infrequently

A team usually meets according to a set calendar. A mission-focused team, on the other hand, meets as often as is necessary to get the task done.

Deflecting Responsibility

Traditional teams often separate authority from responsibility, and this is deadly. Team members end up with a low sense of responsibility for their decisions, and those who do the work often lack the authority needed to make responsible decisions. Mission-focused teams, on the other hand, tend to keep responsibility and authority closer together.

Forgetting about Uninvited Guests

There are always invited guests at a team meeting: our brains and our seats. We are supposed to bring ideas and information and sit as long as the meeting runs. The uninvited guests are our emotions, family problems, and personal concerns. Like little gremlins, they sneak in and mess up a meeting by discharging frustrations in speeches on topics totally unrelated to what is really bothering us. In a strong team, there are no uninvited guests. The whole person is invited. We take time to catch up with each other, assess our needs, and then go on to business.

10

The Great Boss as Change Agent

We can't become what we need to be by remaining what we are.

—Oprah Winfrey

Contrary to the conventional wisdom, Charles Darwin never said that survival was for the fittest. Moreover, Darwin never wrote that it was the smartest who would eventually overcome those of lesser intelligence. Darwin's central thesis in *The Origin of Species* and his numerous other writings always came back to another theme: change. "It is not the strongest of the species that survive, nor the most intelligent, but the ones most responsive to change."

As with living creatures, the same is true for organizations. Look around today. The organizations that are doing well in the face of rising uncertainty and seemingly constant unpredictability are those that are best designed to adapt to the future. They may not have been the most financially powerful nor those run by the most ingenious chiefs.

Leading organizations today are the ones that have built the kind of dynamic, malleable culture that can seamlessly transform itself when the need inevitably arises. Rather than fear the complex and the inexplicable, such organizations run toward the unknown and embrace it as an opportunity. They realize that all uncertainties become smaller if you do not dodge them but confront them. Touch a thistle timidly, and it pricks you;

grasp it boldly, and its spines crumble. Organizations that welcome change realize that success can only be achieved through constant change, through discarding old ideas that have outlived their usefulness and adapting others to current facts.

Like successful organizations, great bosses viscerally understand that because changes are going on anyway, the real value is to learn enough about the changes so that the bosses will be able to lay hold of them and turn them in the direction of their goals. The great bosses know that conditions and events are neither to be fled from nor passively acquiesced to; they are to be utilized and leveraged. How is this accomplished? From my experience, great bosses are able to effect real, positive change through the application of five core competencies. Great bosses have the courage to challenge the status quo; stoke the fire of creativity; manage risk, not avoid it; recognize the necessary role of conflict; and develop new change agents.

HAVING THE COURAGE TO CHALLENGE THE STATUS QUO

Not facing up to the inevitability of change almost always means an inability to suspend the function of the imagination. Fear of challenging the status quo comes from uncertainty. When, on the other hand, we are certain about things, we become almost impervious to fear. Many of the bosses I observed as a young manager were fearful of following their deepest instincts. I saw their careers as safe, expedient, and thin. They made little or no impact and were easily expendable the next time the economy downturned or the company reorganized.

John Wayne once said, "Courage is being scared to death—and saddling up anyway" (Davis, 2003, p. 314). For somebody, anybody, in an organization to step up and challenge what everyone else views as acceptable is tough, real tough. New opinions are always suspect, and usually opposed, for no other reason than that they are not common. This fundamental reality does not deter the great boss. They viscerally understand the resistance to and the inevitability of change. They also understand that standing in the same place for too long is the same thing as dying a slow death.

Great bosses comprehend that no one reaches a high position without daring and courage. They embody the idea that the mighty oak was once a little nut that stood its ground. As Helen Keller observed,

> Security is mostly superstition. It does not exist in nature, nor do the children of men as a whole experience it. Avoiding danger is no safer in the long run than outright exposure. Life is either a daring adventure, or nothing. To keep our faces toward change and behave like free spirits in the presence of fate is strength undefeatable. (1991, p. 122)

STOKING THE FIRE OF CREATIVITY

Albert Einstein said, "Imagination is more important than knowledge" (Folsing, 1998, p. 329). Nevertheless, too often we seem obsessed with analysis and statistics. People everywhere seem to practice the belief that if we could just analyze things a bit more or get some additional data, somehow we would arrive at all the right answers. Although analysis can play an important role, it kills spontaneity. Remember, once grain is ground into flour, it will never germinate again.

Britannica Online defines creativity as "the ability to make or otherwise bring into existence something new, whether a new solution to the problem, a new method or device, or a new artistic object." As a young manager, I remember looking around and seeing so many bored, deer-in-the-headlights bosses that I said more than once to myself, "If that's what being a boss is all about, then no thanks." It is so tempting to fall into sameness. I still see it happen every day.

It is far too common to observe bosses who ignore new ideas and thoughts and do the same thing week after week, and people—not surprisingly—grow tired of it. Any organization and the people who lead it must be creative because people need it. How will any organization grow and mature if it is stuck in a rut?

The great bosses stoke the fire of creativity both in them themselves and in the people around them. They recognize that no great thing has ever been accomplished without creativity. But this does not mean that a great boss should foster an environment of creativity simply for the sake of creativity. An atmosphere of unguided and uncontrolled creativity can be as destructive as a stale one.

Great bosses stoke the fire of creativity in a disciplined way. First, great bosses endorse and support ideas that have potential as the creative solution for a problem the organization faces. Without the endorsement or support of the boss, potentially creative solutions generally die. Second, great bosses establish parameters. This helps those involved in the process to have a clear idea of where to go in their creative wanderings.

Creativity can have a dark underbelly. If not kept in its proper place, it can spin wildly out of control. And even with the best intentions, problems will most certainly arise and mistakes will be made. Accept that and do not let fear of failure paralyze you. Learn from your mistakes and move forward. Here are few ways to better ensure that creativity is both fostered and harnessed in an effective manner.

Stay on Message

A few years ago, a good friend invited me to go with him to watch a heavyweight fight in Las Vegas. I could not help but notice the signs. They are everywhere: big signs; little signs; blinking, flashing, moving signs; even talking signs. It was dazzling. *They don't have a lot to say, but they definitely know how to say it,* I thought. It's too often the opposite inside many organizations. We have so much to say, but we do not always know how to say it. We fail to communicate with our people in a way that is compelling. If an idea does not serve to underscore the theme, then it is not necessary. If you have to explain it too much, then it is probably a distraction, and best avoided.

Do Not Break the Bank

It is easy to get excited about creative ideas and start throwing cargo-holds of money at them, but it is better to involve the people around you. It is a fallacy that you have to be a big organization with deep pockets to be creative. In many ways, creativity can be more intimate in a smaller environment.

Do Not Underestimate the Difficulties
Surrounding Creativity

Creativity is fun. It turns the boring and routine into something challenging and exciting. At the same time, creativity is draining. The process of implementing a creative idea takes an enormous amount of time, thought, and energy. For me, there is nothing so demanding as thinking creatively. It requires both commitment and a tireless work ethic.

Flee the Shallows of Creative Sameness

It is possible to get stuck in a rut even while being creative. Doing the same "creative routine" every time gets mundane too. Great bosses always spice things up with something new.

Navigating without a Map

Creativity naturally involves risk-taking, but make sure that what you do is relevant and within moral and ethical bounds. I would not use certain words, phrases, or movie clips, no matter what kind of point they could make. Some illustrations, controversial or in poor taste, are not worth the fallout. Great bosses must draw the ethical map and make the creative coordinates clear.

MANAGING RATHER THAN AVOIDING RISK

Risk is everywhere. It is all around us—in the bathtub, on the drive home, in our food. Risk is an uncertainty that affects our welfare and is most often associated with loss or hardship. Because risk is inevitable in living our lives and there is no way we can get away from it, we try our best to manage it. We put rubber mats on the floor of the bathtub to get better traction. We wear seatbelts. We try to make sure the food is clean and properly cooked before we eat it. However, despite our efforts to manage risk, we still have to accept that it exists.

For organizations, like all other human endeavors, ascertained risk is managed risk. Generally speaking, when we establish the amount of risk in a given situation and implement ways to reduce the uncertainty surrounding it, we ultimately lower the level of risk associated with the event. Consequently, managing risk involves choosing among various alternatives to reduce the effects of risk.

Managing risk is *not* avoiding it. Instead, it involves finding the best available combination of risk and return given an organization's capacity to withstand the effects of risk. Great bosses and change agents anticipate outcomes as well as plan strategy and tactics in advance, given their likelihood, not merely reacting to those events after they occur. At its core, managing risk—like being an effective change agent—is proactive.

RECOGNIZING THE NECESSARY ROLE OF CONFLICT

Challenging the status quo and stoking the fire of creativity will inherently lead to conflict. There is no doubt about it. Some people will fight a move to change things because it threatens their existence within the organization. Others will view such actions as a power play meant to advance the interests of the change agent. Still others will disagree with the direction the changes are taking the organization. Needless to say, being a great boss in times of severe conflict can challenge the boss's utmost resources and character.

Conflict is the confrontation between differing expectations, purposes, goals, values, or desires and/or the competition for limited resources. Though often unwelcome, conflict is a part of any organization. Sometimes it is good. Other times it is destructive. In the aftermath of conflict many extraordinary and remarkable things can occur. Still, it becomes very important throughout conflict for the great boss to persevere. The word "persevere" is interesting in that after the prefix "per-" is the word "severe." That's what perseverance is—the ability to endure the "severe."

DEVELOPING NEW CHANGE AGENTS

Almost every boss says, "People are our greatest resource." But it is not uncommon to find bosses who do not really allow others to develop. I have seen bosses, perhaps unintentionally, do one or more of the following:

- Magnify the risk—"I know you want this job, but remember: If you fail, you're out."
- Minimize the reward—Instead of talking about the sheer joy of accomplishment, they emphasize the drudgery. "How does your spouse feel about your not coming home for dinner? There will be a lot of nights you'll be working."
- Create a threat—"You really don't like people criticizing you, do you? As a boss, you're going to have to get over that. Everybody in this place gets criticism."
- Show a lack of confidence—"I doubt you're really the right person, but we haven't got anybody else. Somebody has to fill the job." Because every person beginning a job has never done it before, it is easy to tell somebody he or she is not qualified.
- Expect results too soon—"In a couple of weeks, you ought to be on top of this job." The person knows he or she cannot get on top of the project in two weeks; the boss knows it too.
- Deny support—"I'm not going to be able to give you much help. You're going to be out there by yourself."
- Create an atmosphere of criticism—"You can't do anything right." Nobody wants to work for a boss who takes all the credit and transfers all the blame.
- Overstate the effort required—"You probably won't have any leisure time anytime soon. You'll go home with a headache, and your back will ache. That's the price we pay."
- Suggest peer rejection—"You're not really a people person, and this is a people job. But I'm willing to give you a shot at it."
- Emphasize the pressure—"The last person in this job couldn't take the heat." Leaders who do not want others to grow assure them that failures will be fired.

Even if you are not making these mistakes, developing new change agents is tough because people willing to be developed are pretty scarce. There are just not a lot of them out there. On top of that, it is tough to build a team with change agents. You cannot herd cats, and you cannot herd change agents. They are strong-willed and usually have their own vision. Then, if all this were not enough, good change agents are hard to keep. They will be continually enticed with other opportunities that appear to be more exciting and meaningful.

Investing in people is like investing in stocks. High risk can bring a huge return or a huge loss. The greatest change agents will help you the most but can also hurt you the most. They can leave your organization and go to a competitor. When we embrace people and develop them, they will sometimes hurt us. But the future of your organization and your capacity as a great boss depends on developing others to be change agents.

MAKING CHANGE WORK

The mere possession of these competencies is not very valuable unless it is placed into a framework for dealing with change. From my experience, a simple, five-step process can enable a change agent to work his or her people to effectively make changes to the organization.

Step 1—Define the Issue.

What is the problem? What is the real issue? Can it be summarized in a single sentence or two?

Defining the issue may be hard work. Writing it down takes discipline. Getting agreement takes time. But without such definition and agreement, a good decision is unlikely, and successful implementation may be impossible.

Step 2—Get the Facts.

Once the problem is defined, the next step is assembling the facts so that we can be as objective as possible. It is rarely possible to get all the data to guarantee 100 percent accuracy; it takes too long, and some information is just not available. Like the members of a jury, we must learn what we can in order to make our best decision "beyond a reasonable doubt."

Usually the fact-finding step begins with a list of research assignments. Doing those assignments often leads to a longer list because we discover how little we knew at the start. This step continues until enough data has been gathered to underpin a comfortable decision with predictability of success. Again, try to manage risk here and ascertain it.

Step 3—Consider the Alternatives.

Through the process of defining the issue and getting the facts, alternatives will naturally appear. Typically, new alternatives trigger new research, and new research triggers new alternatives. Although direction is necessary all along the way, it is crucial at this stage. The alternatives should be tested against the moral principles of the organization, requirements of the organization, cost, and data collected.

Step 4—Make the Decision.

Despite everyone's eagerness to reach this point, however, deciding can be very difficult. This is where the conviction of the great boss as a change agent takes over.

Step 5—Do It!

Implementation is the final, critical step. Recognize that some will not own a decision until they actually participate in it, so there should be minimum delay between deciding and doing. Do not wait for everyone to agree.

11

Putting It All Together

The final test of a leader is that he leaves behind him in other
men the conviction and will to carry on.
                                        —Walter Lippmann

Two hundred years ago, Thomas Jefferson commissioned
Meriwether Lewis and William Clark to find the source of the
Missouri River, and from there to discover a relatively easy water
route west to the Pacific. Such a waterway, they discovered, does
not exist. But they did succeed in mapping the Northwest, and,
15 months after they began pushing themselves upstream, they
found, near today's Montana-Idaho border, the source of the
mighty Missouri.

Lewis's journal records that on August 12, 1805, a member of
the expedition, Private Hugh McNeal, "exultantly stood with a
foot on each side of this little rivulet and thanked his god that he
had lived to bestride the mighty and heretofore deemed endless
Missouri." The Missouri at its source looks a lot different than the
powerful current that flows into the Mississippi River near St.
Louis.

Likewise, the role of a boss has broadened significantly over
the past decades. And although many tributaries have contrib-
uted to the currents, being a boss is essentially the same river. As
Private McNeal discovered, standing astride the rivulet can be

exhilarating, but he was also more than eager to ride the broader current all the way home.

At the beginning of our journey together, I revealed that my goal for you, the reader, was to see you become one day a great boss yourself. To do that, you must first believe that you can do it. Becoming a great boss is attainable.

Before we go any further, however, let me caution you again about trying to reinvent the wheel. Whereas some pioneers have blazed new trails across formidable frontiers, the vast majority who tried failed abysmally. Trying to reinvent things in the business world is often very expensive and a poor allocation of talent, treasure, and time. Instead, the best bet toward unveiling success is to follow a path that has already been forged. Everything you want, need, and must have in order to achieve your goals has already been invented, perfected, and tested. All you really need to do is uncloak it!

The great questions you need to ask yourself are: *Who* are the people ahead of you on the path to where you want to go? And, *how* are they are getting there? If you can answer these two questions, you too can attain a proven recipe for success.

I wrote this book to give you some guidance for this undertaking. The core competencies that form the basis of being a great boss are simple, yet powerful ways to better organize, operate, and promote yourself. In many ways, they are ingredients for success. Understanding the critical role of doing the right things for the right reason; setting your expectation higher than your boss's; never making the same mistake twice; going to your boss with your action plan, not your problem; and following up—all give us tremendous perspective and insight into what has already worked for those who have preceded us. The outcomes—being a great boss, a great team builder, and a great change agent—are the results. They are the consequences of choices that are made with the idea of becoming better. This is the essence of being a great boss.

KEEPING THE SHIP RIGHTED

It does not take too long to realize that the world we live in is full of cynicism and disenchantment. Even those individuals that could be labeled as great bosses are constantly fighting to keep their ship sailing in the right direction. In order to stay on course and keep their ship righted, I have found that great bosses are always evaluating and reevaluating the ways they things get done. Such individuals realize that success is fleeting and, without determined vigilance, it can all slip away quite quickly. Great bosses regularly query themselves when it comes to how the relationships they enjoy with the people around them stand up.

FOCUSING ON OUTCOMES INSTEAD OF ACTIVITIES

For me, the worst thing that could happen after you read this book is to have you envision being a great boss as merely a set of activities you "do" in order to get along better. Certainly there are necessary steps that each boss must take to move closer toward greatness. Doing the right thing for the right reason is one example.

However, being a great boss is much more than simply doing three or five or even fifty things. Being a great boss is profoundly about showing people a better way to think when it comes to serving employees and customers. Let me elaborate:

Once upon a time, there were two beekeepers who each had a beehive. Their customers enjoyed their honey, and as a result both decided to grow their business. Now as so often happens, the beekeepers had different ideas about how to meet their goal and designed different ways to improve the overall performance of their hives.

The first beekeeper established a bee performance management approach that measured how many flowers each bee visited. At considerable cost to the beekeeper, an extensive measurement system was created to count the flowers each bee visited. The beekeeper provided feedback to each bee at midseason on his individual performance. The beekeeper created special awards for the bees who visited the most flowers. However, the bees were never told about the hive's goal to produce more honey so that the company could increase honey sales and meet their customer's needs.

The second beekeeper also established a bee performance management approach, but this approach communicated to each bee the goal of the hive for ultimately serving their customer's wants and desires. The beekeeper and his bees measured only two aspects of their performance: the amount of nectar each bee brought back to the hive and the amount of honey the hive produced.

The performance of each bee and the hive's overall performance were charted and posted on the hive's bulletin board for all the bees to see. The beekeeper created a few awards for the bees that gathered the most nectar. But he also established a hive incentive program that rewarded each bee in the hive based on the hive's overall honey production. The more honey produced, the more recognition each bee would receive.

At the end of the season, the beekeepers evaluated their approaches. The first beekeeper found that his hive had indeed increased the number of flowers visited, but the amount of honey produced by the hive had dropped. The Queen Bee reported that because the bees were so busy trying to visit as many flowers as possible, they limited the amount of nectar they would carry so they could fly faster. Also, because only the top performers would be recognized, the bees felt they were competing against each other for awards. As a result, they would not share valuable information with each other that could have helped improve the performance of the entire hive (like the location of the flower-filled fields they had spotted on the way back to the hive). As the beekeeper handed out the awards to individual bees, unhappy buzzing was heard in the background. After all was said and done, one of the high-performing bees told the beekeeper that if he had known that the real goal was to make more honey, he would have worked very differently.

The second beekeeper, however, had very different results. Because each bee in his hive was focused on the hive's goal of producing more honey, the bees had concentrated their efforts on gathering more nectar in order to produce more honey than ever before. The bees worked together to determine the highest nectar-yielding flowers and to create quicker processes for depositing the nectar they had gathered. They also worked together to help increase the amount of nectar gathered by the poorer performers. The Queen Bee of this hive reported that the poor performers either improved their performance or transferred to hive #1. Because the hive had reached its goal, the beekeeper awarded each bee his portion of the hive incentive payment. The beekeeper was also surprised to hear a loud, happy buzz and a jubilant flapping of wings as he rewarded the individual high-performing bees with special recognition.

Although it somewhat simplifies the difference between concentrating on outcomes instead of activities, this story illustrates the importance of measuring and recognizing outcomes that really make an impact (honey production) versus activities (visiting flowers).

Activities are the actions taken to produce results. They are generally described using verbs. Examples of activities include filing documents, writing software programs, and doing inventory. In the beekeeper fable, the activity was visiting flowers.

Outcomes are the products or services—the results—of employee and organizational activities. They are generally described using nouns. Examples of outputs include customer files that are orderly and complete, a customer service program that works, and accurate guidance to employees that is friendly and accessible. Outcomes are the final results of all of a company's products and services.

A lot of companies I observe and work with are working hard to develop employee performance plans that support the achievement of organizational outcomes. They would do well to try the second beekeeper's approach of sharing information about organizational goals with the hive, measuring and rewarding accomplishments as well as activities, and providing feedback on performance.

We are not machines that have no choice in how we react to situations. We possess the freedom to choose how we act. Our hearts, minds, and souls combine emotions and intellectual responses to a stimulus so that we can choose our preferred approach. This means that we move from being victims of the situations and circumstances that come our way to empowered human beings who can turn things around. Being a great boss is intrinsically proactive in making the choices about where the organization is heading and how it will respond to the challenges faced along the way. Great bosses are not only proactive themselves, but they build a proactive attitude within the organization.

Appendix: Internet Resource Guide

The following is a list of Internet Web sites that relate to the practice and study of being a great boss. The list is invariably eclectic and is limited due to space. If you have any comments or suggestions that we might take into account for future editions, please send them to us at info@definingthereallygreat.com.

ORGANIZATIONS

Advancing Women in Leadership
www.advancingwomen.com

American Management Association
www.amanet.org

Association of Leadership Education
www.aces.uiuc.edu

Center for the Advanced Study of Leadership
www.academy.umd.edu

Center for Creative Leadership
www.ccl.org

Center for Exceptional Leadership
www.exceptionalleadership.com

Community Leadership Association
www.communityleadership.org

Consortium on Global Leadership
http://sa.hbs.edu/global

Council of Women World Leaders
www.womenworldleaders.org

Government Leadership Institute
www.govleaders.org

Institute for Leadership Research
http://ilr.ba.ttu.edu

Kravis Leadership Institute
http://research.mckenna.edu/kli

Leadership Dynamics Research Institute
www.ldri.com

Leadership for a Changed World
www.leadershipforchange.org

Leader to Leader Institute
www.pfdl.org

Lead International
www.lead.org

National Leadership Institute
www.umuc.edu/prog

Next Generation Leadership
www.nglnet.org

Public Health Leadership Institute
www.albany.edu/sph

Reflective Leadership Center
www.hhh.umn.edu/centers

W.K. Kellogg Foundation
www.wkkf.org

PUBLICATIONS AND E-ZINES

EmergingLeader.com
www.emergingleader.com

Fast Company
www.fastcompany.com

Journal of Leadership
www.baker.edu/departments/leadership

Leadership Quarterly
www.elsevier.com

Leadership Studies Journal
www.lead-edge.com

Positive Impact
www.positiveimpact.org

The Really Great Boss E-Newsletter

Written and published by M. David Dealy and Andrew R. Thomas.

A free, monthly e-newsletter that provides news, summaries, analyses, insights, and commentaries on being a great boss. Written in a similar style to this book, the e-newsletter provides timely updates to issues confronting bosses, interesting links, breaking news, and general commentary. Join the over 10,000 readers who get *The Really Great Boss E-Newsletter.*

To subscribe, please visit http://www.DefiningtheReallyGreat.com.

Privacy policy: M. David Dealy and Andrew R. Thomas will NOT use the e-newsletter mailing list for any other purpose than e-mailing the newsletter. We will NOT use the mailing list for product marketing, nor will we sell the list to any third parties.

Bibliography

Abels, Jules. *The Rockefeller Billions: The Story of the World's Most Stupendous Fortune*. New York: Macmillan, 1965.

Allen, James. *As a Man Thinketh*. Los Angeles: Devorss & Co., 1983.

Buffett, Warren E., *New York Times*, July 24, 2002.

Burns, James MacGregor. *Leadership*. New York: Harper Collins, 1978.

Carnegie, Dale. *How to Win Friends and Influence People*. New York: Pocket Books, Reissue Edition, 1990.

Chamberlain, Joshua Lawrence. *"Bayonet! Forward": My Civil War Reminiscences*. Gettysburg, PA: Stan Clark Military Books, 1994.

Covey, Stephen. *Principle Centered Leadership*. New York: Simon & Schuster, 1992.

Darwin, Charles. *The Origin of Species*. New York: Gramercy Press, Reissue Edition, 1998.

Davis, Ronald. *Duke: The Life and Image of John Wayne*. Norman: University of Oklahoma Press, Third Edition, 2003.

Folsing, Albrecht. *Albert Einstein: A Biography*. New York: Penguin, 1998.

Ford, Henry. *Today and Tomorrow*. New York: Productivity Press, Reprint Edition, 1998.

Godin, Seth. *Survival Is Not Enough*. New York: Touchstone Books, 2002.

Goleman, Daniel. *Emotional Intelligence*. New York: Bantam, 1997.

Hesselbein, Francis, Goldsmith, Marshall, and Beckhard, Richard, eds. *The Leader of the Future*. San Francisco: Jossey-Bass, 1996.

Hock, Dee. *Birth of the Chaordic Age*. San Francisco: Berrett-Kohler, 2000.

Holt, John W., Stamell, Jon, and Field, Melissa. *Celebrate Your Mistakes*. New York: McGraw-Hill. 1996.

Johnson, Spencer, and Blanchard, Kenneth. *The One-Minute Manager*. New York: Penguin Putnam, 1983.

Keller, Helen. *Story of My Life*. New York: Bantam, Reissue Edition, 1991.

Kotter, John. *Leadership Factor*. New York: Free Press, 1998.

Maxwell, John. *Developing the Leader Within You*. New York: Thomas Nelson, 2000.

Melendez, Sara. "An Outsider's View of Leadership," in Hesselbein et al., eds., *The Leader of the Future*. San Francisco: Jossey-Bass, 1996.

Phillips, Donald T. *Lincoln on Leadership*. New York: Warner, 1993.

Pincus, J. David, and DeBonis, Nicholas. *Top Dog*. New York: McGraw Hill, 1994.

Taylor, Frederick. *The Principles of Scientific Management*. New York: Dover Publishers, 1911.

Weems, Lovett H., Jr. *Leadership in the Wesleyan Spirit*. Nashville, TN: Abingdon Press, 1999.

Wittgenstein, Ludwig. *Culture and Value*. Chicago: University of Chicago Press, Reprint Edition, 1984.

Wurman, Richard. *Follow the Yellow Brick Road*. New York: Bantam Doubleday, 1992.

Index

About the Authors

M. DAVID DEALY is Vice President of Transportation for Burling-ton Northern Santa Fe Railroad. A twenty-five-year veteran of railroad operations, he has served in top-level positions in oper-ations and marketing thoughout the industry.

ANDREW R. THOMAS is the bestselling author of several books, including *Aviation Insecurity* and *Global Manifest Destiny*. He serves on the international business faculty of the University of Akron.